CISTERCIAN STUDIES SERIES: NUMBER ONE HUNDRED FIFTY-FIVE

Guigo I

Meditations

CISTERCIAN STUDIES SERIES: NUMBER ONE HUNDRED FIFTY-FIVE

The Meditations of

Guigo I, Prior of the Charterhouse

translated with an Introduction

by

A. Gordon Mursell

Cistercian Publications
Kalamazoo, Michigan — Spencer, Massachusetts

Guigo [I], fifth prior of la Grande Chartreuse, died 1136.

The editors of Cistercian Publications
express their appreciation to
John Leinenweber
for his help in preparing this manuscript for publication.

The work of Cistercian Publications is made possible in part
by support from Western Michigan University to
The Institute of Cistercian Studies

Library of Congress Cataloging in Publication Data:

Guigo I, Prior of the Grande Chartreuse, 1083?–1136.
    [Meditationes Guigonis prioris Cartusiae. English]
    The meditations of Guigo I, prior of the Charterhouse /
translated with an introduction by A. Gordon Mursell.
        p. cm. — (Cistercian studies series ; no. 155)
    Includes bibliographical references (p. 197–99) and index.
    ISBN 0-87907-555-4 (alk. paper).
    ISBN 0-87907-655-0 (pbk. : alk. paper)
    1. Spiritual life—Catholic Church—Early works to 1800.
2. Catholic Church—Doctrines—Early works. 3. Carthusians—
Spiritual life—Early works to 1800. I. Title. II. Series.
BX2180.G7513   1995
242—dc20   94-21178
                                                            CIP

To Sister Benedicta Ward SLG

Acknowledgments

I am extremely grateful to Sarah Goudge for extensive help and advice in the work on this translation; and to Simon Tugwell OP, Dom Bruno Sullivan and others for many helpful criticisms and suggestions. I am also much indebted to Sister Benedicta Ward SLG for her generous advice and comments on the Introduction; and to the late Dom Maurice Laporte and the late Canon Gaston Hocquard, both for their personal encouragement and advice, and of course for their own labors over Guigo's *Meditations*, which has made my own work immeasurably easier.

My greatest debt of gratitude, however, is to Dom Guy Thackrah, formerly Prior of Saint Hugh's Charterhouse, Parkminster, England, who spent many long hours carefully checking and commenting on every word of my translation, and has consistently encouraged me to continue and complete it. Without his constant help and support it would doubtless long ago have been abandoned. I cannot be too grateful to him, even while accepting myself full responsibility for any errors that remain.

Finally, I wish to acknowledge my indebtedness to John Leinenweber and Rozanne Elder, who scrutinized my translation closely and made a large number of invaluable suggestions—and to Dom Bruno Holleran, of Saint Hugh's Charterhouse, whose careful perusal of my efforts brought to light errors both semantic and theological which would otherwise have gone unnoticed.

Gordon Mursell

TABLE OF CONTENTS

INTRODUCTION

Note Throughout this Introduction, references to individual Meditations are given in parentheses and arabic numerals thus (89).

THE AUTHOR

IN 1084 BRUNO of Cologne, former master of the cathedral school at Reims, founded the hermitage of the Chartreuse with a small group of companions, and with the active support of the diocesan bishop, Saint Hugh of Grenoble. Guibert of Nogent has left us a graphic account of what happened:

> After Bruno left the city [Reims], he decided to renounce the world too, and shrinking from the observation of his friends, he went on to the region of Grenoble. There, on a high and dreadful cliff, approached by a rough and rarely used path . . . he chose to dwell, and established the customs by which his followers live to this day. The church there is not far from the foot of the mountain, in a

7

little fold of its sloping side, and in it are thirteen monks who have a cloister quite suitable for common use but who do not live together in claustral fashion like other monks. They all have their own separate cells around the cloister, and in these they work, sleep and eat . . . They are governed by a prior; the Bishop of Grenoble, a very religious man, acts in place of an abbot or director.[1]

The fledgling community, a carefully worked-out synthesis of the eremitic and the cenobitic life, survived the departure of its founder in 1090 (to act as adviser to Urban II in Rome); and in 1109, aged about twenty-six, Guigo (or Guy) was elected its fifth prior. The single most important source of information about his life, as with that of Saint Bruno, is the 'Magister' Chronicle, much of which was written by Guigo himself.[2] The section relating to Guigo is probably the work of Guigo's successor Saint Antelm, though conceivably by his successor Basil.[3] The text reads:

John [of Tuscany] was succeeded by Guigo, from the town of Saint-Romain in the diocese of Valence. He was born of distinguished parents, and was immensely erudite in both secular and sacred studies. He had a keen mind, a sure memory, and a remarkable eloquence, and was very effective in encouraging others, such that none of his predecessors surpassed him in either reputation or authority.

He committed to writing the rule of the Carthusian life, and illustrated it by his example, and, by divine grace, was found worthy of having many disciples in this same order. Under his rule the houses of Portes, Écouges, Durbon, Sylve-Bénite, Meyriat and Arvières were founded and grew considerably both in persons and in buildings, by the mercy of God. . . .

In the last year of his life, and under his direction and counsel, the hermitage of Mont-Dieu was established through the agency of Odo, a very venerable man, who was abbot of Saint-Rémy in the archdiocese of Reims.

Guigo either built from new or restored to their original state almost all the buildings of the upper and lower houses of the Chartreuse. He also built a stone aqueduct, a work of wonder and ingenuity.

He brought a tireless zeal, too, to the careful study, copying and correction of books by proven authors: indeed he wrote in an elevated style the life of blessed Hugh, bishop of Grenoble, at the order of Pope Innocent. . . .

Thus, approaching his fifty-fourth year, the thirtieth after his entry into religion and the twenty-seventh of his priorate, and during the course of the fifty-third year after the foundation of the hermitage of the Chartreuse, our prior brought to an end his holy studies and godly work, and commended his spirit to the Lord on the 27th July.[4]

The other significant source for Guigo's life is a short passage in the life of Saint Antelm,[5] whose author devotes ten lines to a eulogy of Guigo:

There had been at the Chartreuse a prior worthy of eternal fame: Guigo, a venerable man who, by virtue of the mellifluous learning conferred upon him by God, won the privilege of being called the 'good prior' by those who spoke of him. It was he who determined the rule of the Carthusian Order and its permanent boundaries. For he himself put in writing this rule, which he called 'Customs'. He formed those submitted to him, teaching them by word and example. He was concerned, characteristically and vigilantly, to rule with sobriety, honesty and scrupulousness in respect of all that pertained to his office, giving fruitful advice to all who consulted him. He was also a prudent man, remarkable for his mental agility.

We know nothing further about the birth, childhoood and studies of Guigo, though the latter were obviously extensive in view of his subsequent literary activity. In 1106, aged about twenty-three, he entered the Chartreuse and was elected prior only three years later: he held this office until his death in 1136.

The period of Guigo's priorate was one in which the Chartreuse was transformed from an isolated eremitical foundation into the mother-house of a burgeoning order. Such a transformation could not have taken place had it not been for both the energy and ability of Guigo and the unfailing support of Hugh I, Bishop of Grenoble, whose lengthy episcopate enabled him to be both founder and protector of the young community until his death in 1132.[6] Guigo's own *Life of Saint Hugh*, written at the request of Pope Innocent II in 1134, reflects the affection and respect in which he held the bishop: the various extant acts concerning the Chartreuse during Guigo's priorate demonstrate the debt owed by the Carthusian monks to their patron.[7] Guigo's priorate witnessed an event which could have caused the premature death of the young community—an avalanche on 30 January 1132, mentioned in the 'Magister' Chronicle.[8] Furthermore, Guigo's own health was indifferent for much of his life. None of this prevented him from a series of remarkable achievements: the setting-down in writing of the Customs observed at the Chartreuse,[9] a scholarly edition of the letters of Saint Jerome,[10] and considerable intellectual activity. The extent of this is hinted at in various sources, notably in what remains of the correspondence between Guigo and Peter the Venerable of Cluny.

The letters of Peter the Venerable tell us a great deal about Guigo, as well as making it very clear that their friendship was unusually close. Of the two extant letters from Peter to Guigo, the first provides us with the only information we have about Guigo's reading, and will be referred to later. It also reflects their close friendship:

> To the venerable lord and father Guigo, to him whom I embrace in my arms with sincere love, and to his brothers . . . When I try to express in words the profound affection in my heart for you, I confess that I lack the

means to do so. . . . When may I say that, while being
separated from you in body, I am united with you in
spirit, and that, though living elsewhere, I am always
with you . . . ? I have sent you a cross with the image
of the Saviour, so that, being crucified for him in this
world, contemplating him on his cross, and praying for
your own salvation and that of a great number, you may
never forget me in your holy prayers. Let Christ be the
sign of our friendship, and just as the memory of our
Saviour is never far from the sanctuary of your heart,
so too, if possible, let the wretchedness of your servant
never be far from your affection . . . The whole of our
community salute you with a devoted heart . . . [11]

Peter's second letter to Guigo is a moving letter of condolence
following the avalanche of 1132.[12]

Only a short letter from Guigo to Peter has been preserved.[13] In it Guigo introduces himself as 'worthless servant
of the poor Carthusians', thanks Peter for sending a crucifix
to those who, like him, are devoted to the cross, and asks him
not to continue calling him 'father', as he prefers 'brother',
'friend', or even 'son'.

Peter's affection for Guigo also appears in an important
letter to Saint Bernard, which quotes the letter from Guigo to
Peter referred to above.[14] In it, Peter describes Guigo as 'out-
standing in his generation, the most distinguished flower of
the religious life'. In a letter to Milon, bishop of Thérouanne,
Peter compares the pastoral wisdom of Guigo with that of
Saint Augustine:

It was not in this way that bishop Augustine . . . preached
to the people . . . It was not thus that the first fathers and
masters of the churches of God acted; and it was not thus
(to cite someone among the remarkable men of our time)
that Dom Guigo, prior of the Chartreuse, acted . . . in
making known a fault only to the person who committed
it, whereas good things . . . he would announce to all.[15]

Peter's own love for the eremitical life, and his respect for those who lived it, appears frequently in his writings.[16] Like Saint Romuald, Saint Peter Damian, Saint Bernard and others, he loved the contemplative life and lived in a constant tension between that and the more active responsibilities he could not avoid. This is even more true of Saint Bernard, whose extant correspondence with Guigo consists of two letters. The first of these forms the last four chapters of Bernard's treatise *De diligendo Deo*.[17] The second, much shorter, letter extant from Bernard to Guigo refers to his own weakness and ill-health, and probably dates from 1133.[18]

One theme pervades Saint Bernard's correspondence with Guigo and other early Carthusians: the need to be free from external interference so as to be able to be utterly devoted to the life of prayer. No one, not even Peter the Venerable, felt more keenly than Bernard the tension between a longing for God in solitude and an almost compulsive involvement in ecclesiastical and secular affairs. Guigo was himself subject to the same tension, as his extant correspondence reveals. Like Bernard (whose *De laude novae militiae* was to be crucial to their success), Guigo wrote encouragingly to Hugh, Grand Master of the Knights Templar, wishing him and his confrères 'complete victory over the spiritual and corporal enemies of the christian religion, and peace in Christ our Lord.'[19]

Three years later Guigo wrote to Innocent II during his visit to France. The letter reached him during the council of Reims in October 1131. In it, Guigo does not hesitate to give stern advice to the pope, reminding him that he must use only the spiritual weapons of the Lord. He also attacks the followers of the antipope Anacletus II, one of whom is singled out for special venom:

> What has induced Gerald of Angoulême, who has grown old in iniquity, to stand up so impudently and obstinately against catholic peace and truth, if not an inveterate greed and an ambition aroused by the devil's suggestions?[20]

Guigo's letter to Duke William of Aquitaine has a similar theme, exhorting him to renounce his support of Anacletus. Guigo stresses the divine origin of the Church, which 'is alone the body of Christ; only it lives by the Spirit of Christ';[21] and by renouncing it, he warns, William risks the dangers of eternal punishment.

But it is Guigo's letter to Cardinal Aimeric [Haimeric], friend of Saint Bernard and chancellor of the Roman curia, which exemplifies supremely this tension between contemplative withdrawal and secular involvement. Guigo recalls with gratitude Aimeric's visit to the Chartreuse, when he interrupted

> so many and such great ecclesiastical affairs, which never leave you, to make your way humbly and with great effort to our retreat, so as to encounter us face to face and speak with us personally.[22]

Guigo blames the schism in the Church on 'our faults', but nevertheless asks how the Carthusians could possibly pray for divine anger to be averted if they lived in luxury,[23] and continues with a prophetic fire reminiscent of Jerome:

> In the manner of Amalek, inundating the church's domains with a countless multitude of men and animals, we have filled everything, destroying whatever we touch; and, not content with that, we despoil tables, crosses, chalices and holy images. And why? To feed the poor, perhaps, to build monasteries, to redeem prisoners? Not in the least: rather to hire archers, slingers, knights and lancers, so that they can kill Christians and take away the goods and the lives of those for whom they ought to have given their own. What a tragedy! Today, throughout the whole world, following the example of the sovereign pontiffs, brother is hired and armed against brother— that is, Christian against Christian—with holy money; and mother Church congratulates herself at such triumphs, and afterwards, with her conscience soaked in

blood, offers the holy sacrifice. If this is to be endured, then what are we to condemn?

But these practices, they say, are those of emperors in a palace. We do not deny it. Yet if only they had stayed forever in palaces, not in sanctuaries; or better still, if only they had never existed, either in palaces or in churches! How much better it would have been if the Church had given laws to the palaces, rather than the palaces to the churches! Must the churches be taught by the palaces, and should they not rather be entrusted with the task of teaching them? Have the palaces given Christ to the churches, rather than the churches to the palaces? How much more just it would be if kings were to adopt the use of hair-shirts, rather than our adopting their purple! How much more profitable it would be if they assumed our poverty, our fasts and our humility, rather than our taking on their greed, their pleasures and their arrogance![24]

To claim that Guigo's participation in the affairs of church or state was on anything resembling the scale of Saint Bernard's would be foolish; but it is significant that life at the Chartreuse offered no immunity from current controversies. The solitude of the monastery did not entail exclusion from the affairs of the Church. On the contrary, it offered a new and distinctive authority with which to contribute to them. Yet that authority in turn depended on the preservation of the rigorous separation from unnecessary worldly entanglements to which Guigo returns constantly in his writings, and which forms a central feature both of the *Consuetudines Cartusiae* he compiled, and of the *Meditations* translated in this book. For Guigo, the Carthusian vocation was not so much a flight *from* the world as a flight *for* it: the contemplative monk who addressed himself to secular concerns from his monastic solitude saw himself not as someone interfering in matters that did not concern him, but as someone who had the advantage of a clearer and surer perspective from which to view them.

The Meditations: Nature and Style

What did Guigo mean by 'meditation'? In the *Consuetudines Cartusiae*, he twice associates meditation with *subtilitas*: in the Bible, he tells us, people sought solitude when they wanted 'to meditate more deeply on something' (*subtilius aliquid meditari*);[25] and he later extols the 'depths of meditation' (*subtilitates meditationum*)[26] that are attainable only in solitude. Meditation, it appears, has to do with probing to the heart of the matter—a concern with the marrow of meaning, as Guigo described the solitary life in his letter on the subject.[27] In the concluding eulogy of the *Consuetudines* he cites Genesis, in which Isaac 'went out alone into a field to meditate';[28] Saint Bernard cites the same text in his *De consideratione*.[29] Another twelfth-century Carthusian writer, John of Portes, invites his brother to meditate on the mystery of man's redemption and, having done this, to 'open the eyes of his heart, and burn with love'.[30] Bernard of Portes similarly sees meditation as prayerful reflection on the scriptures with a view to discerning God's will:

> After psalmody or prayer, you must meditate on the law of God, especially in the morning, according to the grace that he himself will give you: examine in the secret of your heart what God commands you, and how you can accomplish it; and direct the strength of your heart and your actions to follow the rule of the divine commandments and the example of the holy Fathers.[31]

It is clear that *meditatio* is here primarily a matter of attentive and prayerful reflection on the scriptures with a view to discerning God's will—both a ruminative focussing on a given text, with a concern to probe its innermost meaning, and a wide-ranging reflection on its implications. Jean Leclercq has shown both of these to be ingredients of monastic meditation in the Middle Ages[32], though it is notable that for the late twelfth-century Carthusian Guigo II (who is much more concerned than Guigo I to show the interrelation between meditation and the other three rungs of the spiritual ladder—prayer, reading, and contemplation) *meditatio* is really preparation for prayer: it is still a matter of pondering the sacred text and of going to the heart of its meaning (*interiora penetrat*)[33], but it ranks beneath prayer and contemplation as being something even pagans can do.[34] For the earlier Carthusians, including Guigo I, meditation is clearly one of the distinctive fruits of the solitary life, as well as one of the means by which external concerns are kept at bay: Guigo stresses the need for the procurator, harassed with administrative preoccupations, to return regularly to his cell to calm the turbulent movements of his soul by means of reading, prayer, and meditation.[35]

Meditation, then, may begin with the scriptures; but it does not end with them. The term can also imply a more wide-ranging reflection for which scriptural rumination forms the primary starting-point: John of Portes, for example, invites his brother Stephen to meditate on the God who was made man, and to imitate him;[36] and Augustine had used the word to describe the means by which he employed the 'storehouse' of his memory for fruitful reflection;[37] both Saint Bernard[38] and Peter of Celle[39] commend meditation on death and eternal life; and Hugh of Saint Victor describes the practice of *meditatio in moribus* as being a concern with 'every movement which arises from the heart'—with where it comes from and whither it is going.[40] This latter sense in particular is close to the kind of meditation that characterizes Guigo's own collection. His *meditationes* are precisely what Hugh describes as being concerned both with the end and the direction of all human behaviour;[41] and he shares Hugh's concern for a right intention in all action.[42] Indeed the *Meditations* of Guigo could legitimately be described as an illustration of Hugh's little treatise in its entirety: Guigo's work combines the three kinds of meditation listed by Hugh (*in creaturis*, *in scripturis*, and *in moribus*),[43] although the various distinctions and classifications beloved of Hugh overlap and combine throughout Guigo's work. In the work itself, the word *meditatio*, or its cognates, appears only twice. The first reference, in Meditation 390, will be discussed below. The second occurs in Meditation 407, in which Guigo compares human beings to bricks placed temporarily in a yard (that is, in this world) prior to their transfer to their proper resting-place:

> A person who clings to this yard [i.e. this world] with his heart's affection, rather than taking the trouble to reflect constantly (*semper sollicitus meditatur*) on the place to which he is to be transferred from here, is stupid, not to say insane.

The *Meditations* of Guigo consist of a series of reflections, some related to those around them but others standing on their own. They take the form of a spiritual journal whose primary focus of attention is Guigo's own experience and inner self, which are in turn frequently seen within the context of scriptural truth. The word 'journal' would be misleading, however, if it were to imply either a narrowly individual composition designed exclusively for personal use, or a series of reflections consisting mainly of narrative or even moralizing material. The text certainly reads as though it were primarily for Guigo's own use. Yet the manuscript dissemination, together with the fact that it was copied by monks whose principal literary preoccupation consisted in the copying of manuscripts in the interests of preserving and propagating texts of recognized wisdom and orthodoxy,[44] suggests that it was conceived, or at least edited and written down, with a view to a wider (though certainly monastic) audience. Nor does the text comprise material of a primarily narrative or moralizing nature. Quite apart from the final series of meditations (numbers 464-76), which comprise a theological *tour-de-force* that both summarizes and underlies all that precedes it, Guigo has no interest in separating the rigorously theological from the moral or the personal: indeed it would never have occurred to him, any more than to any other medieval writer, to do so. Christological and experiential reflection blend harmoniously in a single whole.

In none of this is he particularly original. The extensive use of scriptural allusion, and its appropriation for one's personal situation; the even more extensive use of one's own experience and memory; the preoccupation with interior feelings and intentions; the interweaving of the everyday and the eternal, the moral and the rigorously theological—all these features are to be found not only in the works of Hugh of Saint Victor and other contemporary writers, but in texts as widely known as the *Confessions* of Augustine. What *is* original in Guigo's text is, first, his style; secondly, the particular way in which he carefully and precisely interweaves theology and personal experience; and, thirdly, the relationship between the central ideas of the *Meditations* and the actual living-out of the Carthusian vocation. The third of these features forms the central theme of my own earlier study,[45] and needs no further exploration here. The second is discussed later in this Introduction. The first requires a brief elucidation here. Despite the difference in literary genre, the style of the *Meditations* is strikingly consistent with that of Guigo's later works. He avoids every unnecessary elaboration or periphrasis, to such an extent that at some points his intended meaning is not clear. He rarely quotes explicitly, apart from the Bible, and when he does his interest is not in textual precision but in illuminating a particular issue or experience. He is unrelentingly ascetic, though this asceticism needs to be seen in the context of the theology and spirituality which underlie it. He is unsparing in his searching self-criticism, yet without any of the florid and even self-indulgent articulations of personal sinfulness which occasionally afflict writers of this genre.

Nonetheless the style of the *Meditations* is not simply a kind of hyper-asceticism. Guigo evinces a love of pithy antitheses (*Prosperitas* and *adversitas* in Meditation 25; *prosum* and *possum* in Meditation 476; *laboriosus* and *laborare* in Meditation 50, and so on). Perhaps the most striking example of this occurs in Meditation 363, where in ten precise sets of antitheses Guigo contrasts Christ's action in respect of the angels with his action in respect of human beings:

	angels	human beings

          angels   *human beings*

                  Christ

1. leads them to the embrace — snatches them from their
   of their spouse [Christ] — adulterer [the world]
   makes them strong and steadfast so that they can
2. enjoy the spouse — be set free from their adulterer
   holds them fast
3. in sight or reality — in faith and hope or reality
   gives them
4. perfect joy in true happiness — patience in tribulation
5. a happy life — a precious death
6. the right to live for him — the right to die to the world
   [God]
7. joy in their good deeds — grief over their evil deeds
8. joyful hearts — contrite hearts
9. justice — repentance
10. the perfection of goodness — the beginning of goodness

Almost every word is carefully and precisely chosen: indeed some texts, such as 471 and 476, form such *tours-de-force* of structural precision and theological depth as to be remarkable even in the light of their Augustinian sources.[46] A simpler but no less characteristic example is the opening of Meditation 295, where the four nouns used to define love are each in turn annulled by four verbs:

Dum corpus et corpora diliguntur, amor qui est vita, lux, libertas, immensitas quaedam, moritur, obtenebratur, ligatur, angustatur . . .	As long as someone loves the body and physical things, the love which is life, light, freedom and a kind of boundlessness dies, is darkened, bound fast, and constricted.

Or the luminous simplicity of Meditation 77:

Haec redemptio nostra: dimissio peccatorum, illuminatio, accensio, immortalitas. Haec omnia Deus noster nobis.	This is our redemption: forgiveness of sins, enlightenment, being set aflame, eternal life. For us our God is all these things.

Furthermore, Guigo is constantly drawing his own attention to the significance of apparently routine events. Texts frequently begin with *vide, ecce, cogita*, or with stark imperatives or bald statements of fact. The images he uses, though rarely original, are always telling: he shows great pastoral wisdom in the numerous texts in which he compares his role as prior to that of a doctor caring for patients; and the striking image of God as a nurse caring for her child and longing for it to be truly happy (Meditation 454).

Finally, the work abounds with references to the most mundane aspects of everyday monastic life—the cold, the fleas, the smelly goats, the blackberries—and, much more importantly, to perennial and painful struggles with temptation of every kind, and the constant determination to see and explore everything that happens and everything that exists in the context of the *quasi bina dilectio*—the love of God and of neighbor— which is, for Guigo, the only *affectus* by which the human heart should ever be stirred, and the only motivation that must ultimately endure.

THE MEDITATIONS: TEXT AND MANUSCRIPTS

The history of the text of Guigo's *Meditations* is a remarkable process of discovery for which much of the credit belongs to André Wilmart.[47] A very small number of manuscripts survive, but the *Meditations* reappeared, grievously truncated, in six manuscripts from the fifteenth and one from the sixteenth centuries, most of which are from Belgium and Germany. Wilmart suggested that they became popular in Carthusian monasteries in lower Germany during the early fifteenth century,[48] but the (Carthusian?) editor arranged them in an artificial classification and omitted nearly half of them. This partially dismembered text appeared in various subsequent editions, eventually finding its way into Migne's *Patrologia*.[49]

Étienne Gilson had published a translation of sixty-two meditations from the Migne text in *La vie spirituelle*,[50] but

Wilmart was the first to study the original text, and establish it on the basis of the early manuscripts.[51] He identified the manuscripts as follows:

G (Grenoble, Bibliothèque municipale, MS 219 (Catalogue no 264); a twelfth-century manuscript from the Grande Chartreuse. It originally came from MS 195 (Catalogue no 859), which contained a huge collection of ancient christian authors, especially poets (Juvencus, Sedulius, Arator, Prudentius, and Avitus). The *Meditations* appeared in MS 219 between the *De laude castitatis* of Avitus of Vienne and five short works of Boethius.[52]

T (Troyes, Bibliothèque municipale, MS 854); a twelfth-century manuscript from the abbey of Clairvaux, part of a large collection of texts. The *Meditations* are clearly ascribed to Guigo and marked with the Clairvaux *ex libris*: it was presumably copied from a text sent from the Chartreuse and now lost.[53] The suggestion of Gilson,[54] supported by Wilmart,[55] that Saint Bernard must have known the *Meditations* of Guigo through this copy, and that he was referring to it in his letter to Guigo, is not as well founded as Bernard's words at first suggest:

I received the letters of your Holiness with a delight equalled only by my longing eagerness for them . . . How great must have been the fire burning in your meditations to have sent out such sparks as these![56]

Meyer and Smet have argued convincingly[57] that the reference to *meditationes* in Bernard's letter is in fact part of a quotation from Psalm 38:4 (*Concaluit cor meum intra me et in meditatione mea exardescit ignis*). This manuscript is in fact likely to be posterior to Guigo's death,[58] even though it is entirely possible that Saint Bernard, having been informed of the existence of these *Meditations*, did then request a copy to be sent to him.[59] In this case MS 854 would date from somewhere between 1136 (the death of Guigo) and 1153 (the death of Bernard).

M (Munich, Clm. 11352, from the twelfth century). This forms part of a volume from the Augustinians of Polling in Bavaria: the second part of the same volume dates from the eleventh century and includes *Psalmorum flores* and other devotional prayers. The writing is similar to that used for manuscripts at the Chartreuse in the twelfth century.[60]

B (Berlin, Staatsbibliothek, ms Hamilton 89, from the twelfth century). This manuscript contains about fifteen texts of various kinds that could have been intended for teaching clerics.[61] They are the same, and in the same order, as *T* above.

P (Paris, Bibliothèque nationale, ms latin 458, from the fifteenth century). This beautiful manuscript, which belonged to Charles of Orléans (1391-1465), also contains works by Saint Anselm, Hugh and Richard of Saint-Victor, and Jean Gerson.[62]

The text in Migne, usually called *E*, dates from the fifteenth century and, quite apart from omitting half the *Meditations*, has no fewer than four hundred seventy-two distinctive readings: it is manifestly a poor copy.[63]

Wilmart's suggestion[64] that manuscript *G* is in fact a second reading by Guigo himself is supported by Hocquard[65] on the grounds that the *Meditations* give the impression of having been revised and extended by their author. This is possible but difficult to prove: as Laporte has shown,[66] the differences between *G* on the one hand and *M* and *T* (which Wilmart argues were Guigo's first edition) on the other suggest stylistic improvements by a copyist rather than revision by an author.

In all five manuscripts, a small number of initial capital letters are enlarged and decorated in the text, implying divisions that are original.[67] In addition four of the manuscripts (*M*, *P*, *T* and *B*), which appear to have a common source different from *G*[68] have some additional capital letters that are enlarged and decorated.[69] Yet none of these divisions appear to conform to any logical or thematic division within the *Meditations*, one even interrupting the logical sequence of thought.[70] Laporte's suggestion[71] that they may represent new ideas of Guigo, written down at odd moments over the years and faithfully reproduced by copyists, seems the most likely hypothesis; and the fact that most of the capital letters appear in all the manuscripts in the same places implies that the order of the *Meditations* is the original one. If, as is possible, Guigo wrote down his thoughts as they occurred to him, without intending to turn them into a literary production for external consumption, we should not be surprised to find some degree of repetition; and the capital letters may simply indicate new ideas, or points at which he paused. We may reasonably conclude with Laporte[72] that we can to some extent ponder the process whereby Guigo came to write as he did. In this translation, the decorated initial letters which appear in manuscript *G* are indicated by a bold initial letter, thus: **N**-. Of the manuscripts, *G* is evidently the best: its faults are easy to correct by reference to the other four, though in most cases where *G* differs from the others, its reading is to be preferred.[73] Laporte's edition, based primarily on *G*, is critical and reliable: there are very few places where I have questioned his reading.[74]

Finally, no division separates one Meditation from another (with the exception of the capital letters) in the original manuscripts. The numbering from 1 to 476 was the work of Wilmart; and, although on occasion his division appears confusing and arbitrary, all subsequent scholars have adhered to his numbering for the sake of convenience.[75]

DATE AND AUTHENTICITY. The authenticity of the *Meditations* is most convincingly demonstrated by internal evidence. The style is remarkably similar to that of Guigo's other works, and is distinctive, as will be seen. Furthermore there is one meditation in which Guigo refers to himself: Fields, walls, houses, meadows, woods, vineyards and other things of this world ought to want you, Guigo, to fulfil your wishes, for that is to their advantage. This is because you desire and work to improve them, either by adding what they need and will do them good, or by changing them for the better. But you, Guigo, should not want things to turn out as you wish. . . . (Meditation 375).

Both style and content here suggest that the *Meditations* are a kind of spiritual journal. Meditation 455, however, refers to a contemporary event: the quarrel between Count Guigo (Guy) III of Albon and Bishop Hugh of Grenoble, which ended in 1116.[76] More important still, however, in determining authenticity are the innumerable references throughout the *Meditations* to Guigo's role and responsibilities as prior, and to the Carthusian life.

Some of the Meditations, together with the relative lack of emphasis on aspects of the Carthusian life which were to preoccupy Guigo greatly in later works (such as solitude and poverty), give the impression of someone who was relatively new as prior: this, and the reference to a contemporary event which can be dated before 1116, combine to suggest that the whole work dates from early in Guigo's long priorate, probably between 1109 and 1115.[77] It is possible, as Wilmart suggests, that some of the meditations which precede no. 133 (in which Guigo appears to refer to his election as prior) may predate it.[78] Hocquard suggests that the first sixty-four Meditations may come from this earlier period.[79] It is in any case a remarkable work for someone in his early thirties, even if he may subsequently have extended or altered his original thoughts.

LITERARY FORM AND SOURCES

Guigo's Reading

Apart from the evidence of the *Meditations* themselves, a number of other works provide us with information about the nature and extent of written material available to Guigo at the Chartreuse, and thus about the possible sources of his thought and style.

The correspondence between Guigo and Peter the Venerable of Cluny has already been referred to. Of the two extant letters from Peter to Guigo, the first[80] provides us with the only information about Guigo's reading available to us from external sources:

> I have sent you the *Lives* of Saint Gregory Nazianzen and Saint John Chrysostom as you requested. I have also sent you the little work of Saint Ambrose against Symmachus . . . but I have not sent you the treatise of Saint Hilary of Poitiers on the psalms, because I have found in our copy the same textual fault that is in yours. As you know, we do not have the treatise of Saint Prosper of Aquitaine against Cassian, but I have sent someone to Saint-Jean-d'Angély in Aquitaine to look for it, and we will send it to you if necessary. Please send us the large volume of the letters of Saint Augustine, the volume which contains the letters of that saint to Saint Jerome and his replies, because a large part of our copy has been accidentally eaten by a bear in a country house of our abbey. . . . [81]

We have little further information from external sources about Guigo's reading, although Peter the Venerable refers to the importance attached by the Carthusians to the copying of books[82] and Guibert of Nogent mentions the 'very rich library' being assembled by the monks at the Chartreuse.[83] The author of that part of the 'Magister' Chronicle devoted to Guigo tells us that 'He brought an indefatigable zeal . . . to the careful study, copying and correction of authentic books. . . .'[84] And Guigo's letter to prior Lazarus of Durbon, which gives us valuable information about his scholarly work in establishing a critical edition of the letters of Saint Jerome, begins:

> I have been devoting my humble self to assembling and correcting the works of catholic writers which were designed for the instruction of the faithful; among these we have in particular assembled as many as possible of the letters of Saint Jerome, collating them in one large volume, and seeking out and expurgating the faults to the extent to which God has made this possible for us. . . . [85]

The catalogue of the Bibliothèque municipale at Grenoble provides us with valuable information about early Carthusian reading: a considerable number of twelfth-century manuscripts from the Grande Chartreuse survive at Grenoble in spite of numerous fires and other disasters which befell the monastery in the centuries after Guigo's death.[86] Not all of these manuscripts can, of course, be certainly dated from the period of Guigo's priorate; but the contents give us some indication of the material accessible to him and to his successors in the library of the Chartreuse. The preponderance of Saint Augustine is noteworthy: there are twelfth-century manuscripts of his *Enarrationes in Psalmos, De civitate Dei, De Trinitate, De doctrina christiana, De moribus ecclesiae catholicae, De libero arbitrio, De natura boni, De catechizandis rudibus,* and numerous other works, Augustine's exegetical works being particularly well represented. Most of the biblical commentaries of Saint Jerome are present, as well as Gregory's *Moralia in Iob,* the *Vita patrum* (in an early twelfth-century manuscript), and Rufinus' translation of the Rule of Saint Basil. In general, the collection is notable for the large number of scriptural commentaries by various authors, a characteristic confirmed by the early Carthusian homiliary. Compiled for the night office and certainly dating from before 1132,[87] it consists almost entirely of patristic commentaries on the Gospels with relatively little hagiographical material: the texts most used are, in order, Saint Gregory's sermons on the Gospels, Saint Augustine's sermons on Saint John, and the exegetical works of Saint Leo, Saint Ambrose, Saint Jerome, and Saint Hilary.[88]

LITERARY AND THEOLOGICAL SOURCES

(1) Marcus Aurelius and Sextus

In literary and stylistic terms, the *Meditations* of Guigo are unique in the early twelfth century, and no contemporary work which remotely resembles them has yet been found or traced. The most obvious literary comparisons are with earlier works in a similar genre: the *Meditations* of Marcus Aurelius, and the *Sententiae* of Sextus. The former is very similar in structure, consisting of a number of mostly short reflections of a moral and philosophical, but above all a personal, nature. But Marcus' preoccupation with Stoic philosophy contrasts with Guigo; despite Dom Laporte's arguments in favour of some stoic influence on our author,[89] our evidence for this is so indirect and refracted through so many other sources as to defy assessment. Marcus uses everyday experience much less than Guigo does; and in any case there remains the very uncertain question of accessibility, and in particular of whether his work, which was written in Greek, was available to Latin monastic writers in the Middle Ages.[90] The latter, a collection of aphorisms probably written by someone who christianized pagan ideas and reflections,[91] was translated by Rufinus in the fourth century and was certainly popular in the Middle Ages, especially in monastic circles;[92] but the thoughts are even briefer in expression and more aphoristic than those of Guigo, and the similarity of content or style not very significant.

(2) Evagrius Ponticus and the Apophthegmata patrum

In the case of the writings of Evagrius Ponticus, only partially accessible in the medieval west,[93] there is certainly a similarity of style, and occasional similarities of subject matter: both writers are extensively preoccupied with their interior disposition, intentions, and feelings, and with the dangers of self-love; and both relate this internal exploration to substantial theological reflection and principle.[94] But the same could be said of innumerable medieval writers: no explicit references or allusions in Guigo's work suggest any more specific influence. The same can be said of the sayings of the desert fathers. Guigo's brevity of expression, fondness for pithy moralisms, and use of little tableaux and images drawn from everyday life, certainly echo the *Verba seniorum*; and there is one twelfth-century manuscript from the Grande Chartreuse[95] which includes some material from the desert fathers. The influence of texts from the desert pervades every aspect of medieval spirituality; but, as Benedicta Ward has pointed out, the 'desert myth' had a powerful propaganda value for the 'new' twelfth-century monastic orders, much of whose 'return to the desert' was 'tentative and selective'.[96] Guigo wrote within the broad western monastic tradition, which certainly drew inspiration from the desert fathers; but it is for that general inspiration, rather than for specific textual indebtedness, that we should look.

(3) The Bible[97]

Like any medieval monk for whom scripture was intimately familiar from the liturgy, Guigo's writing is full of scriptural allusions, resonances and echoes, which can take many different forms. In Meditation 348 he appropriates a particularly graphic passage to himself:

> The woman who neither fornicates, nor deserts her own husband, simply because she has not discovered an adulterous relationship that will last, is not avoiding adultery but looking for a lasting one. But you, on top of all your wickedness, have mentally stretched open your legs to every passer-by, to enjoy momentary acts of adultery for lack of more enduring or eternal ones.

The imagery here is clearly that of Ezekiel (16:25):

> At the entry to every alley you made yourself a high place, defiling your beauty and opening your legs to all comers in countless acts of fornication. (NJB)

But where the prophet's accusations are addressed to the sinful Jerusalem, Guigo applies the same strictures to himself. On some occasions the scriptural allusion is even more explicit:

> Notice how you love your body incomparably more than it is worth. Your distress is out of all proportion to the harm it suffers. The smallest injury to it, such as a flea-bite, causes you great stress.

But the person for whom God is the entire and sole good mourns the loss of him alone, and nothing else. Not so the rich man in hell: he bore his loss of God lightly, for he didn't ask for God to be restored to him. It was the refreshing water to which he was accustomed that he found hard to be without.

The reference to the story of the rich man and Lazarus in Luke 16 scarcely needs pointing out; and the way in which the deeper significance, the 'marrow of meaning', of the story is applied to Guigo's own spiritual life is entirely characteristic both of the medieval practice of *meditatio in moribus* in general, and of Guigo in particular. Sometimes Guigo, while quoting from the Bible, will change the verbs from the plural to the singular, thereby heightening the sense of the Meditations as personal reflections (see, for example, Meditation 416). Sometimes, too, Guigo's scriptural reflection is less concerned with directly personal application, as in his thoughts about the story of the Fall in Meditation 443. A text such as this might well have served as the basis or distillation of one of the prior's homilies in chapter. Commonest of all, though, are those texts which, while not explicitly alluding to specific scriptural passages, clearly derive from the daily life of monks whose spiritual formation was grounded in the regular reading of the Bible, and in ruminative reflection upon it. This is, as might have been expected, particularly true of Guigo's use of the Psalms: many meditations quote explicitly from them, normally applying the biblical text to Guigo's own life: a brief reflection like Meditation 406 exemplifies the way in which he related the psalms of the monastic office to his personal spirituality.

(4) Saint Augustine and Saint Gregory

The *Meditations* provide us with valuable information about the extent and nature of Guigo's own reading. Occasional classical quotations or allusions, such as a reference to Juvenal in Meditation 147, point to the breadth of his knowledge; and in view of the contents of the extant Carthusian manuscripts referred to above, it is perhaps not surprising to find texts of Augustine forming Guigo's principal patristic source: it would be more surprising if it were otherwise. The nature of his indebtedness will be discussed in section 5 below: much research has been conducted into it.[98] Guigo scarcely ever quotes verbatim, except in one explicit reference to Saint Gregory,[99] whose spirituality also exercised a significant influence on Guigo.[100]

(5) Saint Jerome

One other patristic author deserves comment at this point. We cannot assert with any degree of certainty that Guigo's *Meditations* are directly indebted to Saint Jerome; but both his own edition of Jerome's letters, and his explicit reference to Jerome at the head of the *Consuetudines*,[101] as well as the rigorous asceticism of each—not to mention the love each had for stylistic precision, assonance, and antithesis—suggests that the great Latin father's texts exerted a particular influence on the Carthusian prior. Jerome's scriptural commentaries were widely read and studied in the Middle Ages;[102] and his letters exerted almost as great an influence for their epistolary style and literary quality as for their theological content. A number of certain or probable allusions are given in the notes to the translation. Jerome's emphasis, especially in his classic letter to Eustochium, on a concern for our own interior needs, not on the failures of others;[103] on our persistent predilection for losing sight of what really matters and getting upset over trivia;[104] and, in that and other letters, on the dangers of idolatry— a characteristic theme of Guigo's *Meditations*[105]—suggests an indebtedness of the medieval writer to the patristic one.

(6) Other Medieval Writers

Finally, something needs briefly to be said about the possible influence of other medieval writers on similar themes. The prayers of the eleventh-century writer John of Fécamp[106] are entirely different in style from Guigo's text. But the *Prayers* and *Meditations* of Saint Anselm do form a possible source, even though we have no explicit evidence that a manuscript containing them was at the early Chartreuse. The use of the Bible, the pervasive patristic influence, the preoccupation with the self—all these are (as might be expected) common themes. Occasionally there is a more striking parallel, as with the image of the dog:

Anselm, *Meditation 1*	Guigo, *Meditation 380* (excerpt)
The rotting corpse of a dog smells more tolerable than the soul of a sinful man to God; it is less displeasing to men than that other is to God.[107]	For myself, I would prefer to have the body of a dog than its soul. However, if our bodies were changed so that they resembled those of dogs to the same extent as our souls through wanton behavior come to resemble dogs' souls, who would put up with us . . . ?

The image of God as a husband to whom you are unfaithful, beloved of Guigo, also appears in Anselm (in his second Meditation). But here, as throughout, the style and character of the writing is entirely different, and the similarities of image or content insufficient to suggest any close influence of the one upon the other. More important, perhaps, than any specific allusion is the general approach underlying both texts. Sir Richard Southern has pointed out that it was Anselm, more than anyone else, who established the wide-ranging concept of 'meditation' which was later to be developed by Hugh of Saint Victor as an integral dimension of monastic spirituality, in such a way as to encourage the emergence of works, like his own, in which personal moral reflection (Hugh's *meditatio in moribus*) and more wide-ranging theological enquiry might harmoniously blend. Indeed, as Southern has said, for Anselm enquiry and prayer were indistinguishable, the aim of both being 'to shake off the torpor of the mind and see things

as they are in their essential being'.[108] It is precisely in this
tradition that Guigo's *Meditations* are to be seen; and far more
important than any specific indebtedness of style or content
is the realization that in writing his *Meditations* Guigo was en-
gaged in a fundamentally similar enterprise to that of Anselm
before him, and of his contemporary Hugh. Like them, he
sought to integrate theology with prayer, understanding with
feeling, knowledge with love. In such a context, even the
least movement of the soul or the most trivial antics of the
monastery goat could bear fruit in disposing the monk for
the perspectives of eternity. For a brief and heady period at the
end of the eleventh century and the beginning of the twelfth,
monks such as these were able to combine the everyday with
the eternal in a vivid and remarkably original way. It is in
some respects a cause for regret, at least from the standpoint
of the twentieth century, that later writers came to separate
the one from the other, the theological becoming more aridly
intellectual and the spiritual more introspectively pious.

THE THEOLOGY OF THE MEDITATIONS

Various interpretative approaches to the *Meditations* of
Guigo in recent years have made an important contribution to
our understanding of the text. Georges Montpied,[109] for example, based his thesis on the idea that Guigo's central theme
is the liberation of man, by which he means 'this progress
of the whole being towards freedom';[110] Emilio Piovesan[111]
stressed solitude and silence, as well as the ideas of truth and
goodness, even though the first two of these receive relatively
little treatment in the Meditations; Henri Voilin[112] empha-
sized the centrality of Christ as Truth, and offers some illuminating insights on the theme of love; Maria-Elena Cristofolini[113] offered the important reminder that Guigo's approach
to the world is not as negative as might at first be imagined;
and Guy Hocquard[114] maintained that the matrix of Guigo's
thought is to be found in the twin ideals of beauty and perfection. This incomplete list[115] itself indicates the increasing

interest in this extraordinary work, and the variety of inter-pretations it is capable of supporting. It might also serve as an implicit warning: the *Meditations* are not a work of systematic theology, and there is a danger in offering too organized or coherent an interpretation of something whose primary focus of interest is on the inner movements of the human heart and mind. Nevertheless, the very interrelation of theology and personal reflection they contain allows us to seek to discern the principal ideas and themes on which the work is based.

Self-knowledge and the Use of Experience

The crucial starting-point for any adequate understanding of Guigo's thought must be the author's view of the self, and in particular of the nature and significance of self-knowledge as both a moral and a theological virtue. As we have seen, how-ever, Guigo's view of the self is no narrow introspection. A proper self-knowledge begins with a recognition of one's own sinfulness (Meditation 30); but this sinfulness is not simply a moral problem. It is the direct consequence of the absence of God from within the soul (314); and this in turn results from our own interior and culpable blindness. A recovery of a true self-knowledge is a means, not an end: it enables us to see the truth about ourselves, and thus to begin to change things for the better (162), both for ourselves and for others (142).

The way to self-knowledge, and to a proper self-love, then, lies in a just assessment of the created order and of the place of humanity within it: in an unfaltering willingness to face the truth about ourselves, about other people, about 'the world', and about God. For Guigo, as for Augustine before him, there was an ambivalence about love of self: inasmuch as the self was the source of all enslavement to worldly things, it was clearly to be despised; the more you love yourself, he writes, the more you love worldly things (79). But inasmuch as human beings were also made in the image of God, drawn to ever-increasing conformity to the divine likeness, love of self is manifestly good. One of the ways in which Augustine approached this problem was in relation to the threefold order of creation, a central theme in the final group of Guigo's *Meditations*: the human being assesses himself in relation to God above him, to the human beings beside him, and to creaturely and material things below him; and this offers a criterion for a just assessment.

True self-knowledge leads neither to a grovelling self-abasement nor to a flight from self. On the contrary, the monk is called to dwell within himself (90); and, as Guigo points out in one of his letters, the solitary life requires a mind that is its own master, that is anxious for itself, and that despises a false involvement in the affairs of others.[116] An apprehension of the truth about oneself becomes, in Guigo's theology, the only sure way to perceive the truth about anything at all, and Guigo makes this point with characteristic force (437). Hence the importance of interior transformation above all else[117]— not in order to ignore other people, but precisely in order to be well equipped to help them. People who have little or no knowledge about themselves are highly unlikely to be very much use to anyone else.

The cardinal virtues in this regard, the indispensable preconditions for a true self-knowledge, are humility and patience. Guigo tells himself to concentrate on the interior journey 'on humility or patience', and leave crusading and other exterior journeyings to others (262). In Augustinian spirituality, humility is not only a moral but a theological virtue: by coming to discern your true place in the creation, and the true state of your soul, you are able to respond to God, the world and other people as you should. In this perspective, the solitary life is not a static escape from the world, but a dynamic process, a journey of the soul towards self-knowledge by means of growth in humility and patience—a journey as costly and perilous as any crusade or pilgrimage. The raw material of this interior journey is nothing more or less than human experience, the warp and woof of everyday life. Saint Bernard's famous reference, in one of his sermons, to the task of reading from 'the book of our own experience'[118] is echoed by Guigo in Meditation 192. This is not to say that all experience is somehow good: Guigo simply says that it invariably arouses our feelings (38). He also quotes Saint Paul in saying that 'all things work together for good to those who love God', even the evil deeds of someone else (396). And this enables him to make use, for the purpose of moral and theological reflection, of even the most mundane aspects of everyday experience when it suits him to do so. Perhaps the best example of this is his reflection on an antiphon (282):

> Notice how, when you recently tripped up in front of the brethren by singing one antiphon instead of another, your mind tried to think of a way of putting the blame on something else—on the book, or on some other thing. Your heart was reluctant to see itself as it really is, and so it pretended to itself that it was different, inclining itself to evil words to excuse its sin. The Lord will show you up, and set before you what you have done; and you will not be able to hide from yourself any longer, or to escape from yourself.

The 'you' here is Guigo himself, as Benton notes, 'trying to stand apart from his "heart" or "mind" and to be aware of inner drives of which he had not before been conscious'.[119] But he is also doing more than that: he is seeking to explore the effects of a lack of self-knowledge, effects which hurt others as much as they hurt him; and he is doing so in the context of his own present and potential relationship with God. In the light of the theology that underlies it, this exploration of motivation and experience becomes an integral aspect of growth in the spiritual life, for only when human beings are free to see themselves as they really are can they learn to love God, and their neighbor, as they really should. In this theological context, even the most apparently trivial everyday experiences can be fruitful, and Guigo does not hesitate to use them.[120] In each case his primary concern is not with the experience itself, but with the observation of his own reaction to it, and in particular the assessment and examination of his intention.

The importance of right intentions is stressed by many patristic authors;[121] and Guigo here follows Augustine in employing the image of the doctor, in his case as an analogy for his own role as prior (see, e.g., 151–2). Elsewhere he makes it clear that there is in reality only one good intention—the *caritas consulendi*, the love that seeks the good of others (433). Only when this becomes your motive are you free to rebuke others as well as to praise them, because only then are you free to discern what they need.

Theological Anthropology

Guigo's exploration of the self is only a means to an end. The 'end' is set out in the extraordinary group of texts which form the conclusion to Guigo's work (Meditations 464 to 476), a conclusion so apparently different from the remainder of the text as at first to suggest that it was added later, perhaps even by a different hand. However, not only does every manuscript of the text contain the final group of meditations, but also the difference in style and content is more apparent than real. The rich theological (and particularly christological) focus of the concluding group only serves to underline the *theological* significance of all that precedes it. And the interweaving of personal and theological reflection begins at the very start of the work (see, e.g., 3 and 5) and continues throughout. The final group of texts offers a more developed, though still strikingly concise, theological key that opens up a proper understanding of the whole work.

The final series of meditations begins with a text in which Guigo points out the contrast between the natural beauty proper to the created order, and his own lack of it (464). This affirmative view of creation might appear to clash with his continual ascetic stress on *contemptus mundi*; but here too the conflict is more apparent than real. The problem is not in the world, but in human beings' attitudes and intentions towards it. In the next meditation, Guigo explains what he means by the 'natural beauty and perfection' of a rational creature: it consists in being 'devoted to God' (*devotam esse erga Deum*), and in showing kindness to one's neighbor *usque ad mortem* (465). The link between love for God and love for neighbor here is important, pointing to what in Meditation 390 Guigo calls the *quasi bina dilectio*. Once again, Guigo is making here a profoundly theological, not just a moral, point. Human beings, for him as for Augustine before him, form the mid-point in creation, between God and 'the world'.[122] By learning how to value or assess each 'level' in this hierarchy correctly, human beings discover their own fulfilment. And, since this evaluation is both a cognitive and an affective process, it has to do both with theology and spirituality, with knowledge and love. None of these is to be separated from the others.

In the next Meditation, Guigo sets out the way in which the human person is to relate to 'the higher things'—in other words, to God. Although he does not explicitly make use of it here, his approach to God is that of enjoyment, in its Augustinian sense. In the *De doctrina christiana*[123] Augustine distinguishes between things to be used and things to be enjoyed: those to be enjoyed make us blessed, while those to be used help us to move towards beatitude, so that we can cling to the things to be enjoyed. What is to be used is a means; what is to be enjoyed is an end. We are placed between, in the midst of, both: if we enjoy what should be used, we will be bound by an inferior love; for to enjoy something means to hold fast to it with love for its own sake: to see it as an end, not a means. So God is to be enjoyed;[124] for he is that than which there is nothing higher or more sublime. Yet we could not enjoy God unless God had made himself known, supremely in the Incarnation whereby he appeared to those of weak and impure vision,[125] and by means of which he becomes both our way and our heavenly homeland.

This stress on God alone as the proper object of our love, as the only person whom we should love for his own sake, appears at various points in the Meditations (see, e.g., 198–199); and Guigo constantly underlines the perennial human temptation to make things of the world ends rather than means. He calls this *ydolatria*, loving worldly things for their own sake (or, as Augustine would say, enjoying them). To love God as an end is to love him for his own sake, not for the sake of something else (414). This is not to say that our love for God can ever be entirely disinterested: it is to say that we are to love him precisely because he does not need our love (359); because by doing so we begin to share something of his life and nature (329); and because thereby we are set free from enslavement to the world so that we can love it, and other people, as we should. True love, then, is disinterested: it is its own reward; and it alone makes love of others possible.

This brings us to the true evaluation of human beings which forms the subject of the next meditation (469). Guigo begins by stressing the fundamental equality of all human beings, and the inextricable link between his salvation and that of everyone else. Guigo's pastoral concern for his brothers, which is again and again manifested in the *Meditations*,[126] is grounded in a precise metaphysic: only by apprehending clearly and objectively the place of the human person as midpoint between God and the lower creation, and by assimilating the consequences of this for our relations with our neighbor, is true love possible; for only when the human person is set free from the twin perils of pride (distorting his relationship with God) and of *cupiditas* (distorting his relationship with the world) are we in a position to see others as they should be seen (that is, as God sees them), and so to love them as we should.

Having considered the proper approach to God and to our fellow human beings, Guigo now turns to the 'lower things' (*inferiora*), which he defines as 'those which come after the rational spirit' (470). Nothing is to matter to human beings less than these, as Guigo says unequivocally (470). Yet, although Guigo clearly emphasizes the inferiority of 'the world', it is in itself morally neutral. Worldly things are not in themselves bad: what matters is our attitude to them (366). Elsewhere he suggests that our most appropriate attitude to them is to see them as signs, pointing beyond themselves towards their creator and ours (308, 373). Even so, his primary concern is to warn us against the dangers of inordinate attachment to the world—precisely that, because such attachment overturns the threefold order. This need not prevent people from enjoying the beauties of creation, or (as we have seen) from gaining profit even from the lowliest of creatures; but it does mean that the things of this world are created to point beyond themselves, and that nothing is to be gained by trying to improve them. Efforts of this kind should be directed only to those human beings who are neither perfect nor incapable of change, as Guigo points out, for only they are both capable of amelioration and in need of it (462).

Guigo's attitude to the world is not, however, simply negative, nor is it confined to a theory of 'signs'. There is in the *Meditations* a positive theology of adversity which is a vital ingredient in the monastic life. Like Gregory the Great before him,[127] Guigo antithesizes *prosperitas* and *asperitas*: the first is a 'snare' that imprisons the love of God (25): the second, like adversity in general, is the only sure path towards a proper renunciation of worldly enslavement. Indeed, as Guigo elsewhere says, adversities are adverse only for evil people, for those whose love is wrongly directed (184).

It is important to see the positive value of this approach. A wrongly directed love of the world is for Guigo not really love at all, but idolatry, a favorite theme to which he constantly returns.[128] It results in an inability genuinely to love others, because once our perspective is distorted we cannot discern what constitutes others' good, and (even more important) we are no longer free to love others disinterestedly. This is a vital point: an ascetic approach to the world, properly understood, does not cut us off from our neighbor—on the contrary, it frees us from a false dependence and lets us love them as we should. In turn this frees them from a false dependence on us. Small wonder, then, that Guigo should devote so much stress to the dangers of enslavement to things of this world, an enslavement that represents unfaithfulness to God, our true spouse (241, 278–279).

The Threefold Order

Having set out the distinctive ingredients of our respective relationships with God, our neighbors, and with the 'lower creation', Guigo continues with a summary which is one of the finest things he wrote, and which perfectly exemplifies both the character and the theological depth of his work. Meditation 471 summarizes all that has so far been said in a series of careful and precise statements that deserve detailed exploration, because they enable the entire theology of the *Meditations* to become clear.[129] Structurally, the text may be seen as comprising thirteen sets of human attributes, of which the first seven are triple and the remainder double. The first five of the thirteen form part one of the text, analysing the place of humanity in the created order. The sixth and seventh sets form part two, which is almost entirely negative, and in which man's responses to this order are explored. The remaining six sets form part three, which both synthesizes and extends what precedes it. The structure may be set out as follows:

MEDITATION 471

The human person's attitude to

The higher things *superiora*	The equal things *aequalia*	The lower things *inferiora*
Part One (Sets 1–5)		
1. man's delight *superiora ad gaudium*	man's companions *aequalia ad consortium*	man's servants *inferiora ad servicium*
2. devotion to God *devotus ad Deum*	kindness to neighbor *benignus ad proximum*	circumspection to the world *sobrius ad mundum*
3. servant of God *Dei servus*	companion of man *hominis socius*	lord of the world *mundi dominus*
4. set beneath God *sub Deo constitutus*	not arrogant to his neighbor *erga proximum non elatus*	not subject to the world *mundo non subditus*

5. [order inverted]

| the lower things *inferiora* | Man will restore for the well-being of the middle things *ad utilitatem mediorum* | and the honor of the higher ones *ad honorem superiorum* |

Part Two (Sets 6–7)

6.

| ungodly *impius* blasphemous *blasphemus* sacrilegious *sacrilegus* | Man will not be arrogant *elatus* envious *invidus* bad-tempered *iracundus* | inquisitive *curiosus* profligate *flagitiosus* |

7. [order inverted]

| nothing from the lower *nihil ab inferioribus* | Man will accept nothing from his equals *nihil ab aequalibus* | but everything from the higher *sed totum a superioribus* |

Part Three (Sets 8–13)

8. Marked with the imprint of the higher *a superioribus impressus* — man will mark the lower with his imprint *inferiora imprimens*

9. moved by the higher *a superioribus motus* — he will move the lower *inferiora movens*

10. influenced by the higher *a superioribus affectus* — he will influence the lower *inferiora afficiens*

11. following the higher *superiora sequens* — he will lead the lower *inferiora trahens*

12. possessed by the former *ab illis possessus* — he will possess the latter *ista possidens*

13. restored by the former to their likeness *ab illis in eorum similitudinem redactus* — he will restore the latter to his likeness *ista in similitudinem redigens*

Each of the first four sets of attributes in Part One has a subtly varied grammatical pattern: nouns in the first, adjectives in the second, substantives in the genitive in the third, and past participles ending in *-tus* in the fourth. In each, the place of human beings in creation is developed by a series of precise relations: by finding our delight in God, we are able to keep company with our neighbor, and to be served by the world. By being devoted to God, we can be kind to our neighbor and temperate in our attitude to the world. By being the servant of God, we can be the companion of our neighbor and the lord of the world. By discovering ourselves to be set beneath God, we can be free from arrogance towards our neighbor and from subjection to the world. The two sins consequent upon a failure to apprehend the threefold order are thus arrogance (setting ourselves above our neighbor), and enslavement (setting ourselves beneath the world, or setting the world in God's place). The result of these four is expressed in the fifth, in which a human being becomes the active subject for the first time: we are free, by virtue of our relationship with God, from the twin perils of arrogance and enslavement; and this in turn enables us to use the world positively (Guigo here exceeds anything he has said hitherto about the human attitude to the world): we can bring it back, or restore it, to the good of our neighbor, and the honor of God. This is the virtue consequent upon a proper understanding of the threefold order, and it summarizes Part One of the text as well as being complemented by Part Three. Part Two thus acts as a central pivot, and it comprises a long series of negative statements designed to heighten the impact of the unconditional positive at the end. A true apprehension of the threefold order prevents us from falsifying our relationship either with God (through evil, blasphemy or sacrilege), or with our neighbor (through arrogance, envy or ill-temper), or with the world (through inquisitiveness or profligacy). This can be achieved only by taking nothing from the world, or from the neighbor, *but everything from God*—the inversion of the customary triple order of predicates in set seven merely heightens the significance of this final statement. This unconditional love for God is central to the anthropological structure as a whole, and in turn leads to the final part, which matches and balances the first.

In Part Three, the 'equal things' (our neighbor) are omitted so as to stress the vital role of human beings as mediators between God and the world once our own disposition with regard to both higher and lower things is rightly ordered. This in turn is subtly stressed by the most crucial grammatical point of all: in Part Three the human being is entirely passive with respect to God, and entirely active with respect to the world. This passivity, or receptiveness, before God alone allows us to be creatively active towards the world; and the two principal sins (arrogance and enslavement) are precisely the inversion of this: arrogance implies activity towards God, and enslavement passivity towards the world. This dialectic between passivity and activity is of great theological significance, as the predicates of the last six sets of attributes make clear. By virtue of being marked with God's imprint (or, in more explicitly Augustinian terms, of being made in God's image and potentially in his likeness), we are able to mark the world with his imprint. By virtue of being moved by God, we shall be able to move the world. By virtue of being influenced, or affected, by God, we shall be able to do the same to the world. By learning to follow God, we shall be able to make the world follow us, instead of following it ourselves; and by virtue of being possessed by God, we shall own the world.

Part Three, like Part One, ends with a set of attributes based upon the use of the verb *redigere*. At the end of Part One we saw that, by virtue of being set beneath God, the human person is able to bring the world to the good of his neighbor and to the honor of God. But now we can go further: once we are conformed to the likeness of God, we can conform the world to our likeness (that is, both to our human likeness, and to the likeness of God, since both become the same). Thus the ultimate goal and vision of the threefold order is the perfect conformation of the world to us, and of us to God; and it is attained by a configuration of the human vocation in which we learn first to be acted upon, and then to act: first to receive the unconditional love of God, and then to offer our neighbor and the world the fruits of that love, by which alone they can be redeemed: an active asceticism that derives from a passive openness to the love of God.

All this presupposes a willingness on the part of human beings to fulfil their God-given vocation as mediators, a willingness which Guigo, as well as anyone, knows is only rarely in evidence. After reflecting on the implications of this anthropological schema for the world to come, he therefore proceeds to what is in effect the theological climax of his work, in Meditations 473–474. If we had been able to see (at the deepest level) the truth of the threefold order, we would not have needed a saviour. But, blind as we are, we failed; and so the Word of God became incarnate 'and dwelt with us, in our external world, so that in this way at least he might one day lead us into his inner world' (474). In Christ alone— and here Guigo begins to gather together all the ideas of the final group of meditations—are found to perfection all the attributes already outlined: Jesus fulfils completely the human vocation as it is adumbrated in Meditation 471. He is thus our exemplar, but he is also more than that: he is, so to speak, perfect human nature, incarnating in his life, death, and teaching the essence of the human vocation. What he did by virtue of his intimate personal union with God, we are now able to do by virtue of the sacraments, the teaching, and the example through which his incarnate life is present to us now. And this will mean living as he did, and making our own this rightly ordered love, and this divinely given understanding of the structure of the threefold order, and of the place of human beings within it, which Jesus supremely articulated.

Yet this 'rightly ordered' love introduces an apparent paradox: if we are to love God utterly and unconditionally, how can we also love our neighbor 'even unto death', as Guigo stipulates? Once again, however, the contradiction is more apparent than real, which brings us to perhaps the most important point of all—the crucial relationship between the ascetic and moral life set out in the Meditations and the theology that underlies it. This theology is *in itself* profoundly ascetic: it demands a radical detachment from the things of the world and an unqualified concern for the good of one's neighbor rather than the furtherance of one's own interests, and that not as an end but as a means. Only the renunciation of an inappropriate worldly involvement sets human beings free to enjoy God alone, and thus to love others without seeking dependence, or domination—that is, to love human beings as they should be loved, as God loves them. The process may be put the other way round: by seeking to enjoy God, we discover freedom to love our neighbor and the world as they should be loved. We are free from the need to seek our happiness or salvation through them, which would only result in enslavement to them. This alone enables us to love them in a way which is conducive to our good as well as to theirs.

So, by conforming ourselves to the likeness of Christ, we become in reality what we have always been in potentiality—mediators between God and the world. Guigo concludes his work with a short meditation that is a *tour-de-force* of concise synthesis: though clearly based on texts of Augustine,[130] it serves as a summary of all he has said.[131] And what he has said is at once traditional and remarkable. It is traditional because it stands clearly in the line of western Augustinian theology. But it is also remarkable because what Guigo has done is to show with stark clarity that the logic of such theology points to the monastic life. The rigorous preoccupation with self-knowledge and reflection on experience leads to an apprehension of the truth about God and the creation. God alone is to be loved unconditionally, and nothing is to be preferred to him. Human beings are to be seen in their proper perspective as the midpoint between God and the world, and as equal to one another. They differ from the animal creation both by virtue of their rationality, and by virtue of the image of God which indwells each of them, an image which can be obscured but never entirely lost. If it is not to be obscured, human beings must embrace a proper attitude towards the world, a responsible activity that itself derives from a true *passivity* before God and that shuns any temptation to worldly enjoyment, or to seeing worldly things as ends rather than as means. In turn, too, our attitude towards God determines our attitude towards our neighbor, though the extent of our sinfulness prevents us from perceiving and apprehending this threefold order as we should. Hence the need for the Incarnation, so that in the person of Jesus God might himself make manifest the ultimate implications of the threefold order and provide an exemplar of unconditional yet ascetic love. Human love in its fullest embodiment, then, is to be found precisely among those who might appear to have renounced it unequivocally; and the logical fulfilment of this theology of love is the ascetic life of the Chartreuse.

Cura Pastoralis

Finally, something needs briefly to be said about the pastoral concern found throughout the *Meditations*, a concern which derives its character and motivation from the firm theological foundation from which it derives. In a group of related meditations, Guigo develops the image of the doctor and his patients as an analogy for his own role as prior and his relationship with the monastic community (349–352). The good doctor will do what ought to be done even if the results appear disappointing, for a sick person is committed to a doctor not so that the latter may do what he wants with him, or dominate him, but so that he can heal him. It is as healer, rather than as master, that Guigo envisages his role. Like any good doctor, he must act both with skill and with the right intention; and, even if the results are disappointing, he will be judged to have acted worthily if his intention was a genuine concern for the other's good. He is to hate, not the person, but the sin, just as a doctor hates not the patient but the sickness (346); and in each case his task is to do good (211), not to worry about his own reputation (189).[132]

Guigo defines his task elsewhere as being that of a *utilis socius* (190). Both words are significant. *Utilis*—a word which recurs throughout the *Meditations*[133]—relates to the process of doing good, of being profitable; but it also symbolizes that interweaving of the theological and the practical which characterizes all Guigo's writing. *Socius* is a striking word for the head of the monastery: there is no abbatial grandeur in view here. To be a utilis *socius* means seeking to be taught rather than to teach, to be helped as much as to help (190); it means bearing a burden which is slight when compared with that of Christ (191); it means reprimanding someone, but only out of love for him (*ex caritate qua illum diligas*) (210), as a doctor administers a bitter potion (211). Most of all, it means beginning with yourself (*incipe ergo a te*) (220), admitting that you know yourself very inadequately (*Vide quam te ipsum ignores*) (303), and avoiding above all else the sin of pride (263). In these and many other pithy and perceptive aphorisms Guigo sets out in practice the nature and implications of disinterested love. The pastoral dimension of this love is constantly to the fore, and is in itself striking testimony to the centrality of pastoral care even in so severe and solitary an order—a centrality it was to maintain centuries later.[134] Guigo tells himself to love the potential in people (see, e.g., 142, 167–168), and to avoid at all costs making people dependent on him, even if the logical conclusion of such an ambition is the termination of his own office (195). This pervasive and pastoral sensitivity is perhaps the most purely attractive aspect of the whole work; and it offers a valuable corrective to the otherwise austerely ascetic picture of himself that Guigo offers us. It also points to the conclusion reached above by another and no less valid route: if the logical conclusion of the Augustinian theology of love is the solitary yet monastic life of the Carthusian, then Guigo's Meditations do not just suggest what that means in theory. They offer us hints of a single-minded, uncompromising and scholarly ascetic, with a remarkably sure and coherent sense of what his vocation entailed, of its immense costs and its pastoral implications, of its enduring temptations and its ultimate reward. And, as though by way of a precaution, in case that were not enough

to ensure their lasting value, they also offer us fleeting but
certain glimpses of a genuinely happy man:

Your natural place is to be a good companion and friend
of people, not their proud master. Do everything, therefore, with companionable love, not with overbearing arrogance.

Love must be drunk for its own sake, because of its
own sweetness, like the most delicious nectar. Even if everyone were to go crazy, it is not to be sold at any price.
For love does us good, and makes us happy, whatever
others may do. (150–151)

THE INFLUENCE OF THE MEDITATIONS

The *Meditations* of Guigo appear to have been infrequently
copied at first: only a small number of manuscripts survive,
and these were so little diffused that no contemporary author
seems to have cited them or known of them.[135] Despite its
reference to *meditationes*, and the interesting reflections on
disinterested love, we have already seen that the letter of
Saint Bernard to Guigo offers no evidence that the abbot
of Clairvaux had read or received Guigo's *Meditations*.[136] *The
Meditations* and *Scala claustralium* of Guigo II, ninth prior
of the Chartreuse, might be expected to show evidence of
Guigo I's influence; and Guigo I's reference in Meditation
390 to *contemplatio, oratio, meditatio, lectio* is a possible point
of reference with Guigo II's work. In fact the two are quite
different: where Guigo I is concerned, in Meditation 390,
to relate the different ingredients of 'spiritual exercise' (or,
as he calls it, *opera divinae devotionis*) with those comprising
love of neighbor (*opera fraternae dilectionis*), Guigo II is instead
concerned with the relationship between the four rungs of his
ladder: contemplation, prayer, meditation, reading.[137]

In the middle of the fifteenth century Guigo I's *Meditations*
suddenly reappeared in six manuscripts, but in a grievously
truncated edition which omitted 230 of the 476 meditations

and classified the rest in a highly artificial manner.[138] One at least of these manuscripts came from the charterhouse of Cologne;[139] and Wilmart suggests that this strange edition may have arisen from the German charterhouses at a time when the Carthusian communities there were flourishing and were especially concerned with literary work and the copying of manuscripts—a practice which Guigo himself explicitly commended in his *Consuetudines*.[140] From 1546 onwards this edition, attributed to William of Saint-Thierry and combined with his Meditations (or *Meditativae orationes*), appeared in various places in northern Europe.[141]

Dom Le Couteulx, perhaps the greatest of all Carthusian historians, recorded in about 1680 both this profusion of copies of Guigo's *Meditations* and the existence of a much more complete text in a manuscript at the Grande Chartreuse: unfortunately, however, he says no more about it.[142]

The influence of Guigo's work on later medieval writers is extremely hard to calculate. James Hogg has noted some striking parallels between Guigo's *Meditations* and the *Conclusa* of the fourteenth-century Carthusian Henry of Kalkar, who was closely connected with Geert Groote and the *Devotio Moderna*, and who wrote his work during his priorate of the charterhouse of Monnikhuisen near Arnheim.[143] Both the autobiographical character of Guigo's work and his emphasis on a thoroughgoing *imitatio Christi* would be likely to appeal to the writers of the *Devotio Moderna*.[144] But the severely mutilated form in which the *Meditations* appear to have been circulated makes it virtually impossible to assess their influence on late medieval spirituality. Furthermore, the more explicitly Christ-centered devotion of late medieval piety might be expected to reveal, at best, only indirect influence of works of early twelfth-century spirituality like Guigo's *Meditations*.

NOTES ON THE TRANSLATION

Except where explicitly stated to the contrary, this translation is based on the critical text of the *Meditations* established

by Dom Maurice Laporte and published in Sources Chré-
tiennes volume 308 (Paris: L'Éditions du Cerf, 1983).

Biblical References

Guigo's Latin is economic, vivid, extremely precise, shorn
of all pomp and display, but with its own character and distinctive features. Occasionally the sense, or precise application, of
what he writes is ambiguous or even unclear. He frequently,
and usually implicitly, quotes or makes allusion to biblical or
patristic sources. Finally, notwithstanding the possibility that
even from the start he envisaged others reading his work, his
primary focus of interest in the *Meditations* was himself. These
factors do not make his Latin easy to translate, though they do
give it a distinctive character. This translation is designed, as
far as possible, to preserve that distinctiveness. Where Guigo
alludes to, or quotes explicitly from, the Bible, the translation
does the same, making use in most cases of the Authorized
(King James) Version, as being the version likely to carry the
same resonance and significance for English-speaking readers
as Jerome's Vulgate did for Guigo.[145] The quotations are
rarely precise. Biblical references are given in the notes to
individual Meditations wherever the Bible is explicitly cited,
and in a number of cases where a biblical passage appears to
be the source of Guigo's reflection.

Vocabulary

Vir and *Homo*

Where English has traditionally used 'man' to refer to humankind, Guigo employs *homo*. Only when he refers to a
spouse or husband does he employ *vir*. So far as possible,
this translation has sought to preserve the distinction obvious in Latin but not, until recently, in English. Only in a
few Meditations (notably in Meditation 476, a masterpiece

of dense concision), did I feel that the substitution of 'human being' or 'humanity' for 'man' would ruin the effect of Guigo's brevity.

Pius and *Pietas*

The translation of *pius* and its cognates presents problems: the English 'pious' and 'piety' have less attractive overtones. The use of 'good' and 'goodness' (together with 'wicked' for *impius*) would be one possible option (and is clearly appropriate in Meditation 95); but this lacks the religious connotation that is clearly important in Guigo's use of these words (and which emerges even more clearly in his later *Consuetudines*).[146] In the end I decided to use instead 'godly', 'godliness', 'ungodly', and so on, not only because they seem to catch the sense of Guigo's Latin more exactly, but also because they are almost invariably used in the Authorized Version where *pius* and its cognates appear in the Vulgate. The only exceptions have been where Guigo uses the word to denote 'dutiful', 'conscientious', 'devoted', as in *pius medicus*.

Species and *Forma*

The translation of *species* and *forma* presents even greater difficulties. Both are important words in the writings of Augustine, and their meanings overlap. *Species* may be said to correspond in general to the external aspect of created things, their appearance and (especially) their beauty, though it can also be used to denote the Greek word *eidos*, and thus to designate the divine 'idea' which makes each thing what it is. *Forma* is frequently used for *eidos*: it means intelligible structure, that which confers order and identity on matter (as in Genesis 1 'the earth was without form, and void'). Augustine describes God as the *forma infabricata, atque omnium formosissima*.[147] But he also speaks of *carnales formae* as meaning those physical attributes which can be perceived sensorily, by means of the flesh, and which must be striven against because they detain and distract us.[148] Guigo's use of the word, usefully classified and summarized by Maurice Laporte,[149] refers in almost every case to these *formae corporum* which are perishable and yet perilously attractive to us. The striking exception is Meditation 283, a beautiful text in which *forma* refers to God in all but name, though in Meditation 360 Guigo speaks of people being *formaliter* identified with God. In this translation the word 'form' has been used consistently throughout: neither 'shape', 'appearance' nor 'attribute' offers quite the range of meanings implied in the Latin.

Appetere

The word *appetere* is, as Hocquard has pointed out,[150] invariably a strong word in Guigo's writings, and the translation has sought to retain this in English, albeit with a variety of different words ['to seek eagerly' (12 and 331), 'to seek keenly' (71), 'to crave' (73 and 402), 'to long' (114), 'to set one's heart on [something]' (179, 403 and 461)]. Only in Meditation 199 does the word have a less intensive meaning (here translated 'to seek'). Behind many of Guigo's uses of the word is his own stress upon that "hunger for things which are above" (*appetitio superiorum*) which he refers to explicitly at the end of the *Consuetudines Cartusiae*, and which informs all of his spirituality.[151]

Disciplina

The word *disciplina* is capable of a number of meanings in monastic texts. It can mean 'discipline' or observance in a general sense; but it can also imply the distinctively monastic practice of self-administered flagellation as an act of penance. Both meanings appear in Guigo's *Consuetudines*; and Jean Leclercq suggests[152] that in the *Meditations* Guigo employs it in its second, more technical, sense. The word occurs three times in the text—in Meditations 386, 390, and 392; in 386 it is clearly related to punishment; in 390 it is listed as one of the 'works of brotherly love'; and in 392 it is used in a much more general sense.

Patristic References

It would be tedious and virtually impossible to track down all of the implicit allusions to patristic texts, many of which Guigo would have heard read regularly in the Carthusian night office. In a work of this kind doing so would in any case add little to the reader's profit. The two French translations of the Meditations (by Laporte and Hocquard) both include numerous patristic references, some extremely illuminating and others with only minimal relevance to Guigo's text. In this translation a note has been made of those patristic references which seem to the translator either to be the explicit source of Guigo's words, or genuinely to illuminate our understanding of it.

Notes to the Introduction

1. Guibert of Nogent, *De vita sua*, trans. J. F. Benton as *Self and Society in Medieval France* (New York: Harper Torchbooks, 1970) 60–61.

2. For the text, manuscript history and origin of the 'Magister' Chronicle, see Wilmart, 'La chronique des premiers chartreux', in *Revue Mabillon* March 1926.

3. See Wilmart, p. 62. J. Picard (*St Antelm de Chignin* . . . [Belley: Collections de recherches et d'études cartusiennes, vol. I, 1978], p. 61*) follows Le Couteulx (*A. O.C.* I:xcii) in maintaining that Antelm was the author, stressing correctly the stylistic differences between the notices on the first four priors and that on Guigo I.

4. 27 July 1136.

5. For a detailed discussion of the date of this biography, see Picard, pp. 72*–73*.

6. For a detailed discussion of the significance of Saint Hugh of Grenoble for the early Carthusians from Saint Bruno to Guigo I, see *Aux sources de la vie cartusienne* (published anonymously but written by Dom Maurice Laporte) (La Grande Chartreuse, 1960–71) vol. 2, chapter 2. Saint Hugh was much older than Guigo, and would have been a father-figure for him (Laporte, 36).

7. For these, see B. Bligny, *Recueil des plus anciens actes de la Grande Chartreuse (1086–1196)* (Grenoble: Allier, 1958) esp. the acts numbered XII to XX.

8. For a detailed discussion of this event, see Picard, p. 27* n. 71, and pp. 57*–58* & nn. 19–20.

9. *Consuetudines Cartusiae*, edited with a french translation by a Carthusian (Dom Maurice Laporte) in *Sources Chretiennes* (SC) vol. 313 [1984]). For an extended commentary on the *Consuetudines*, see *Aux sources de la vie cartusienne*, vols. 5–7.

10. This edition has been preserved in Madrid, Biblioteca Nacional, MS 26. For a brief discussion of its significance, see G. Mursell, *The Theology of the Carthusian Life in the Writings of St Bruno and Guigo I* (Salzburg: Analecta Cartusiana, 127 [1988]) 75–77.

11. Ep. 24; ed. Giles Constable, 1:44–47, 12, Ep. 48; Constable, 1:146–48. G. Hocquard, *Les Meditations du bienheureux Guigues de Saint-Romain, 5ème prieur de Chartreuse* (Salzburg: Analecta Cartusiana, 112, 1984) 12, n. 6, suggests that this letter must date from March or April 1132, rather than the curiously vague dating (1122–37) suggested by Constable.

12. Ep. 48, ed. Constable 1:146–48. G. Hosquard (1984, p. 12 n. 6) suggests that this letter must date from March or April 1132, rather than the curiously vague date (1122–37) suggested by Constable.

13. Edited with french translation, by a Carthusian (Dom Maurice Laporte) in SCh 88:206.

14. Ep. 149; Constable, 1:364.

15. Ep. 102; Constable, 1:264.

16. See, e.g., his letter to Gilbert the hermit (PL 189:89–100), and the critical edition by J. Leclercq in *Studia Anselmiana* 40 (1956) 112–20. Even more interesting is the description of the Carthusians in Peter's *De miraculis* (Book II, chapter 28–29; PL 189:943–9).

17. Ep. 11; ed. Leclercq & Rochais *Sancti Bernardi Opera*, 8 volumes (Rome: Editiones Cistercienses, 1957–77), vol. 7:52–60; English trans. by B. S. James, *The Letters of St Bernard of Clairvaux* (London: Burns & Oates, 1953) 41ff.

18. Ep. 12; SBOp 7:61–62; English trans. by B. S. James pp. 48–49.

19. Text and French translation in SCh 88:154–61.

20. Ep. *ad Innocentem* 4; SCh 88:168. Gerald of Angoulême was a bishop who supported Anacletus.

21. Ep. *ad Willelmum* 3; SCh 88:178.

22. Ep. *ad Aimericum* 2; SCh 88:184.

23. *Ibid.* 5; 188.

24. *Ibid.* 7; 190.

25. *Consuetudines Cartusiae* (hereafter CC) 80:4, SC 313 p 288.

26. CC 80:11, SC 313 p 292.

27. *Epistola de vita solitaria* 4, SC 88 p 144.

28. CC 80:5, SC 313 pp 206–8.

29. *De consideratione*, SBOp 3:420–1; english translation by Elizabeth T. Kennan and John D. Anderson, *Five Books on Consideration*, Cistercian Fathers Series 37 (Kalamazoo, 1976)

30. Ep. *ad fratrem suum* 28; SCh 274:134.

31. Ep. *ad Rainaldum inclusum* 10; SCh 274:66.

32. 'Études sur le vocabulaire monastique du moyen âge' in *Studia Anselmiana* 48 (Rome, 1961) 134–5. For the significance of *meditatio* in the benedictine tradition generally, see Adalbert de Vogüé, *The Rule of St Benedict: A Doctrinal and Spiritual Commentary*, (Cistercian Studies 54 Kalamazoo, Michigan: 1983) 135–136, 155 and esp. 242–248.

33. *Scala claustralium* 4; SCh 163:88.

34. *Ibid.* 5; SCh 163:92.

35. CC 16:2, SCH 313:200.

36. Ep. *ad fratrem suum* 19–20; SCh 274:128.

37. *Confessiones* 10:8; Bibliothèque Augustinienne vol. 14:166 '. . . et haec omnia rursus quasi praesentia meditor'.

38. *De consideratione* 5:32; SBOp 3:493.

39. *De disciplina claustrali* 24–5; SCh 240:258–82.

40. *De meditatione* 3:3; SCh 155:52.

41. *Ibid.* 3:5; SCh 155:52.

42. *Ibid.* 3:1; SCh 155:50.

43. *Ibid.* SCh 155:44.

44. See Mursell, pp. 196–202.

45. *Ibid.*

46. See below.

47. See in particular his 'Les écrits spirituels des deux Guigues', in *RAM* 5 (1924) 59–79, 127–58, reprinted in *Auteurs spirituels . . .* (Paris, 1932) 217–60; and his complete text of the *Meditations*, with (rather loose) translation, 'Le recueil des pensées du B. Guigue', *Études de philosophie mediévale* 22 (Paris, 1936).

48. 'Les écrits,' 223. Page numbers for this article refer to its reprinted form in *Auteurs spirituels*.

49. PL 153:602–632.

50. Étienne Gilson had published a translation of 62 Meditations from the Migne text in *La vie spirituelle* 40 (1934) 162–78.

51. *Le recueil des pensées du bienheureuse Guigue* (Paris: Vrin, 1936).

52. SCh 308:76–7. In the Catalogue of Manuscripts of the Bibliothèque municipale of Grenoble these are listed as follows: fol. 1 *Avitus* of Veinne *episcgoi De laude castitatis* fol. 5 Guigo I *Meditationes* fol. 24 Boethius, *Liber quomodo Trinitas unus Deus . . .* fol. 27 Boethius, *Liber utrum Pater et Filius . . .* fol. 27v. (*Incipit ejusdem liber*) fol. 28v. Boethius, *Fidei christiani . . .* fol. 30v. Boethius, *Liber adversus Nestorium*

53. SCh 308:78.

54. *La vie spirituelle* 40:163–5.

55. *Le recueil . . .* 41, 44.

56. Ep. 11; SBOp 7:52; trans. B. S. James,*The Letters of St Bernard*, 41.

57. 'Notes sur quelques sources littéraires relatives a Guigues Ier, 5ème prieur de la Grande Chartreuse' in *Revue d'histoire ecclésiastique* 48 (1953) 194.

58. art. cit. p 195 & n 6.

59. Laporte, SCh 308:80–1.

60. SCh 308:78.

61. SCh 308:81.

62. SCh 308:83–4.

63. Wilmart, *Le recueil*, 45; SCh 308:86–7.

64. Wilmart, *Le recueil*, 43–5; SCh 308:88–91.

65. *Les méditations*, 70.

66. SCh 308:86–7.

67. These appear at the head of м 376, 454, 456, 457, 460, 462, 466 and 473; SCh 308:91.

68. SCh 308:85.

69. Those that contain all four appear at the head of м 39 and м 426; SCh 308:91.

70. At the start of м 466.

71. SCh 308:92.

72. SCh 308:93.

73. SCh 308:94.

74. Specified in the notes to the translation.

75. SCh 308:97.

76. SCh 308:15.

77. SCh 308:15; Hocquard, 42; Wilmart, *Le recueil*, 40.

78. *Le recueil*, 40.

79. *Les meditations*, 42.

80. Ep. 24; Constable, 1:44–47.

81. Jean Leclercq makes the delightful point (*Pierre le Vénérable*, 266) that we must not forget that parchments at the time were made of sheep skins, which would be very attractive for bears!

82. *De miraculis* II; PL 189:945.

83. *De vita sua* XI (ed. Labande) 68 ('*Cum in omnimoda paupertate se deprimant, ditissimam tamen bibliotecam coaggerant* . . .). See also P. Fournier, 'Étude sur la bibliothèque de la Grande Chartreuse au moyen age' in *Bulletin de l'Académie delphinale*, 4th series, 1(1886) 305–86, though Fournier deals principally with the library at the Chartreuse in the fifteenth century.

84. Wilmart, 'La chronique' 50.

85. Text in SCh 88:214.

86. See P. Vaillant, *Les manuscrits de la Grande Chartreuse* . . . (Grenoble: Roissard, 1984) chapter two.

87. For a detailed study, see R. Etaix, 'L'homiliaire cartusien', in *Sacris erudiri* 13 (1962) 67–112.

88. See Mursell, 172ff.

89. See his Introduction in SCh 308:45–48.

90. The wide range of classical, as well as patristic, literature contained in manuscripts deriving from the library of the Grande Chartreuse suggests that so famous a work might have been available to Guigo.

91. See Henry Chadwick, *The Sentences of Sixtus: A Contribution to the History of Early Christian Ethics* (Cambridge, 1959).

92. See SCh 208:33.

93. See SCh 308:35–36.

94. See introduction to SCh 170 and Simon Tugwell, *Ways of Imperfection* (London: DLT 1983) chapter 3.

95. Ms 1172 at Grenoble, Bibliothèque municipale.

96. 'The Desert Myth: Reflections on the Desert Ideal in Early Cistercian Monasticism' in *One Yet Two*, CS 29 (1976) 188.

97. On Guigo's use of the Bible, see L. Giordano Russo, 'Guigo e la Bibbia nelle *Meditationes*' in *Orpheus* 24–25 (1977–78) 187–197.

98. Notably by G. Hocquard, in his invaluable commentary on the *Meditations* published in *Analecta Cartusiana* 112/2 (1987).

99. *Meditation* 294; SCh 308:198.

100. See the Conclusion to my *The Theology of the Carthusian Life*.

101. CC Prol. 2, SCh 313:156.

102. See Beryl Smalley, *The Influence of the Bible in the Middle Ages* (London 1940) esp. 20–22, 41–42, 127–28.

103. Ep. 22.38; ed. J. Labourt (Paris: 'Les Belles Lettres' 1982, vol. 1) 154–156.

104. Ep. 22.39–40; ed. Labourt, 1:156–158.

105. See Ep. 22.10, Ep. 14.5–6.

106. See Jean Leclercq and J. P. Bonnes, *Un maître de la vie spirituelle au xie siècle: Jean de Fécamp* (Paris: Vrin, 1946).

107. Trans. Benedicta Ward (London: Penguin, 1973) 221.

108. Southern, *Saint Anselm and his Biographer* (Cambridge UP 1966) 54.

109. G. Montpied, 'Essai sur la spiritualité cartusienne d'après les Meditations de Guigues l'ancien 5ème prieur de Chartreuse', Diplôme d'études supérieures d'histoire (Grenoble University, 1957).

110. Montpied, 72.

111. E. Piovesan, 'Guigo I: Le Meditazioni', *Analecta Cartusiana* 17 (1973); also *ibid.*, 'Fedelta alla gerarchia delle esseri imitando il Verbo Incarnato', in *Rivista di ascetica e mistica* 1 (1966) 51–60.

112. H. Violin, 'Un penseur méconnu: Guigues le chartreux', in *Bulletin de l'Académie Delphinale de Grenoble*, 8th series, 11th year, 4(1972) 98–117.

113. M. E. Cristofolini, 'Le "Meditationes" del beato Guigo Certosino (+1136)', in *Aevum* 39 (1965) 201–17.

114. 'Les Méditations du bienheureux Guigues de Saint Romain, 5ème

prieur de Chartreuse (1109–1136)', *Analecta Cartusiana* 112 (1984) esp. 60–103.

115. See esp. E. Gilson, 'Présentation de Guigues Ier le chartreux', in *La vie spirituelle* 40(1934), pp. 162–78; A. Wilmart, 'Le recueil des Pensées du Bx Guigue', Études de philosophie mediévale 22 (Paris: Vrin, 1936); Dom Maurice Laporte, Introduction to Guigues Ier, *Meditations*, in SCh 308 (1983) 7–101; and A. Schlüter, *Gigo von Kastell: Tagebuch eines Mönches: Des Karttaüserpriors Gigo Meditationen* (Paderborn, 1952).

116. *Ep. de vita solitaria* 5; SCh 88:144.

117. M 157; M 334; M 354, using a biblical illustration; and M 398.

118. SC 3.1: 'Hodie legimus in libro experientiae'; SBOp 1:14.

119. J. F. Benton, 'Consciousness of Self and Perceptions of Individuality', in *Renaissance and Renewal in the Twelfth Century* (Oxford: Clarendon Press, 1982) 263.

120. See, e.g., M 221; M 265; M 272; and M 306.

121. E.g. Gregory The Great, *Moralia in Iob* 28.31 (PL 76:466), Cassian, *Institutiones* 10.16 (SCh 109:410), Augustine, *Homilia in Epistolam Ioannes* 8.9 (PL 35:2041).

122. See Mursell, 103–4.

123. I.3; CCSL 32:8.

124. I.7; CCSL 32:10.

125. I.12; CCSL 32:12–13.

126. E.g. M 88; M 150; M 190; M 195.

127. *Monumenta Germaniae Historica, Epistolae* 1:207.

128. See, e.g., M 313; M 326; M 369; M 384.

129. Mursell, 125–30. See also Hocquard, *Analecta Cartusiana* 112 (1984) 91–4.

130. Among them *De Trinitate* 7:4, (CCSL 50:253), *Enarrationes in Psalmos* 134.5 (CCSL 40:1941).

131. See Mursell, 134–7.

132. The concept of Christ as doctor is very common in patristic texts; see, for example, Leo the Great, *Sermo de passione* 13.2 (Sch 74:166); and R. Arbesmann, 'The Concept of *Christus medicus* in St Augustine', *Traditio* (1954) 1–28.

133. See Mursell, 138–44.

134. See the interesting article by Vincent Gillespie, 'Cura Pastoralis in Deserto', in '*De Cella in Seculum*: Religious and Secular Life and Devotion in Late Medieval England', ed. Michael Sargent (Cambridge: D. S. Brewer, 1989) 161–82.

135. Introduction to edition of the Meditations published in SCh 308 by 'a Carthusian' (Dom Maurice Laporte), p. 71; G. Hocquard, 'Les Meditations du b. Guigues de Saint Romain, 5ème prieur de Chartreuse', *Analecta Cartusiana* 112 (Salzburg, 1984) 1.

136. See above.
137. See Mursell, 217–237, esp. 235–236.
138. For detailed history see Laporte, Introduction to SCh 308, (71–76); and Wilmart, 40ff.
139. Cologne, Stadtarchiv W.8 535.
140. CC 28.2, SC 313:222. See Mursell, 196–202.
141. Louvain (1546), Antwerp (1548, 1550, 1554, 1589 and 1590), Paris (1600), Luxembourg (1621), and Paris (1680). See Laporte, Introduction to SCh 308:72 & n. 53.
142. *A. O.C.* (ed. Montreuil 1887) vol. 1:416.
143. See J. Hogg, 'The English Charterhouses and the Devotio Moderna' in *Acta* of the 4th International Colloqium on "Historia et Spiritualitas Cartusiensis"' (ed. J. de Grauwe, Belgium: Destelbergen, 1983) 259. For Kalkar, see H. Ruthing, *Der Kartaüser Heinrich Egher von Kalkar 1328–1408.* Studien zur Germania Sacra 8 (Göttingen, 1967).
144. See Hogg, 261.
145. At one point (Meditation 348) Guigo cites the *Vetus Latina* text. Although his biblical citations are rarely exact, the vulgate appears to have been his principal source. The citation from the *Vetus Latina* may have come to Guigo through Jerome, Ep. 96.12. See Hocquard, *Analecta Cartusiana* 112:2 (1987) 62.
146. See, e.g., CC 12.5, or 19.2.
147. *De vera religione* 21, Bibliothèque Augustinienne, vol. 8:52. There is an extremely illuminating *Note complementaire* on the meaning of *species* and *forma* for Augustine in the same volume, pp. 486ff.
148. *Ibid.* 45; BA 8:86.
149. SCh 308:315–318.
150. 'Les Méditations,' 2, Analecta Cartusiana 112.2 (1987) 4.
151. CC 80.7; SCh 313:290.
152. Article 'Disciplina' in *Dictionnaire de Spiritualité*, 3 (1956) cols. 1294–1300. See also Hocquard, 'Les Méditations,' 2, Analecta Cartusiana 112:2 (1987) 66–67.

The Meditations of Guigo,

Prior of the Charterhouse

The Meditations of Guigo
Prior of the Charterhouse

1

Consider how violent are the desires that are aroused in you, not by the Lord but by things which should not even be named, and how more people are possessed by obscene lusts than by the Lord.

Eph 5:3

2

Be ashamed to do what is unseemly for you either to see yourself, or to show to others.

3

You should set truth at the centre of things, as something beautiful. Do not judge someone who abhors it, but have compassion on him. As far as you are concerned, though, if you desire to attain truth, why do you recoil from it when you are reproached for your vices?

4

Consider how much truth must endure. To the drunkard you say, 'You are a drunkard', and likewise to the wanton person and the gossip—and it is true. Yet these people instantly lose their tempers, and persecute the truth in the person of its preacher: they kill him.

But notice how the lie is honoured! 'Good masters!' is said to the worst people, and to the slaves of all the vices. They are delighted: they rejoice, and venerate the lie in the person who speaks in this way.

Mt 23:34

5

Without form or comeliness, and nailed to the cross—thus is truth to be adored.

Is 53:2, Col 2:14

6

Claim your reward from the person whose will you are employed in serving. Live in such a way as to owe nothing to yourself, because you cannot pay anything back to yourself. The Lord says 'Do not keep back the wages of your hired servant until morning.' The Lord will therefore take vengeance on you against yourself.

Lev 19:13

7

A person who does everything according to his own will should demand full payment from himself; and, since he cannot extort it from himself, he should appeal against himself to God, the just judge. If you really loved yourself, then, you would never find pleasure in serving someone—in other words, yourself—from whom you would look in vain for a reward.

Ps 7:12

8

Why do you claim ownership of yourself rather than of some person or land, when nothing in you is any more your handiwork than anything in them is? By what right do you claim for yourself any of the things you have not created any more than you created yourself?

9

Consider how much easier is the way to life through unpleasant things than through pleasant ones. To curb lust and other cravings is easier when nothing beautiful or seductive comes your way.

10

You should not be attached to your own body through delight in it or love for it, in other words through sin, but only by virtue of the fact that you give life to it.

11

Insofar as the Lord, who is the truth, has freed you from love of things which you will lose because either they or you will perish, he has also delivered you from fear of sorrow and from actual distress. And the same applies to being freed from hate.

Jn 8:32

12

Consider the nature of what is good, the last lingering traces of whose footprints—that is, transient things—are eagerly sought after at so great a risk of hardships and bloodshed by so many creatures, rational and irrational alike.

13

Transient need and hardship, like a torturer, forces us to desire instead good things that are quite different from them. But because we have become accustomed only to transient things and know nothing else, we desire things scarcely any different from what is making us suffer now; and we choose either briefly to suspend their rampages, in other words the hardships they cause, alleviating them with some kind of truce, or to submit ourselves to things that are scarcely any different from them.

14

O man, enduring such pain! Would you like to relieve it? 'Yes, I would.' For a while, or for ever? 'For ever.' Then desire eternal relief, that is, God, the truth: for he struck you so that you might desire him, not medicinal herbs or bandages.

15

A person who seeks a long life seeks a long trial: human life upon earth is itself a trial.

Job 7:1. Jerome, Ep 125.7; 'Even the stars are not pure in the sight of God: how much more is this true of human beings, whose life is a trial?' (ed. Labourt, 7:120).

16

You are just only if you recognize and declare that because of your sins you deserve condemnation. If you declare yourself just, you are a liar, and are condemned by the Lord who is truth as being disagreeable to him. Admit you are a sinner, so that you may be a truthful person agreeable to the Lord who is truth, and be set free.

1 Jn 2:4, Jn 8:32

17

You are complacent because you do not understand that you possess nothing good that comes from yourself. From yourself you have nothing but evil. You owe yourself no thanks, then. All evil comes to you from yourself. You owe yourself heavy penalties, then, by way of punishment.

18

Be the sort of person you would praise. Only a good person is really to be praised. Someone who wants to be praised is not good, and so gets no praise.

19

When you flatter someone who praises you, you are not really flattering him for praising you, because you are not really being praised, you vain person! When someone says 'How good and just he is!', the person who really is good and just is being praised—not you, who are no such thing. On the contrary, you are receiving no little censure, you who are so wicked and so unjust: a just person's praise is an unjust one's censure—and so it is yours, as an unjust person. So when you applaud someone who praises a just person, you are applauding one who quite rightly censures you, because you are unjust. Anyone who regards himself as just is not just, not even a day-old infant.

Job 14:4–5 (LXX). Augustine, *Confessions* 1.7; CCSL 27:6–7

20

Anyone who delights in praise destroys it. If you love praise, have no desire for the praise due to a saint; in other words, if you want to be praised, you should stop wanting it. For no one who wants to be praised can truly be praised. The one who is praised is the one whose achievements are renowned: the one who wants to be praised is not only devoid of anything good, but is moreover full of a great and diabolical evil: arrogance. So he is not praised. On the other hand, the just person, who deserves no censure, is invariably praised. Censure is in fact a reproach for what is evil. Now the just person cannot be reproached for qualities that he does not possess. Therefore he cannot be censured. All praise for the just is invariably censure for the unjust, and all censure for the unjust is true praise for the just.

Jerome, Ep 52.5, ed. Labourt 2:180

21

When someone is praised for doing good, it benefits not the one who is being praised but the one who is praising him.

22

Prepare yourself to live in the company of evil people, with your mind unsullied; to do this is to live like an angel. Yet what glory is there in doing this among saints?

Cf. Gregory the Great, *Homilia in Evangelia* 38:7 'If you are good, then, bear patiently with the bad as long as you remain alive. Anyone who does not bear with the bad is a witness against himself through his intolerance that he himself is not good.' PL 76:1286; CS 123:344.

23

Someone who loves everybody will undoubtedly be saved. But someone loved by everybody will not on that account be saved.

24

Just as hating you is a hindrance to life for everyone, so too is hating everyone for you. For you to love everyone is to your advantage, then; and to love you is good for them.

25

Prosperity is a snare: the knife for cutting this snare is adversity. Prosperity is a prison for the love of God: the battering-ram for breaking it open is adversity.

For the antithesis of *prosperitas* and *adversitas*, see Gregory the Great, *Letter to Priscus*, in MGH Epp 1:207. See also Meditations 82 and 183.

26

A single fever carries off everything you struggle against, in other words, the delights of the five senses. What remains, therefore, other than to give thanks to God for giving us the victory? But you, on the contrary, out of your hatred for freedom, are actually looking for something to which you may succumb.

1 Cor 15:57

27

What hope is there if you throw yourself willingly onto the snares and darts of the enemy—if you not only are not wary of them, but even readily embrace them and expose yourself to them? You flee from one to the other; you think of them as a remedy or a comfort; you long for them, and cannot bear to be without them.

28

Adversity prompts you to long for peace; but you, blind as you are, desire something that, for as long as you love and desire it, makes peace completely unattainable.

29

Welcome the truth joyfully, as though it were the Lord himself. But either tolerate a lie with serenity, or refute it.

30

You do not realize that you are bound fast; and you do not struggle against your chains as a dog does.

31

Consider two experiences: swallowing and evacuating. Which makes you happier—what you experience through the latter or the former? The former burdens you with useless things, the latter unburdens you. What good do you get from the two of them? Simply the experience of having completely consumed something! Nothing beyond that remains to be expected from them.

So it is with everything sensory. Consider, therefore, what happiness all such things have brought you, whether in reality or in expectation, and so judge those still to come. Reflect, I tell you, on past pleasures, and so judge those to come. Everything you hope for will perish; and what will you have left then? Love and hope for what does not pass away.

32

You ought not to rejoice at all in yourself or in anything else, but only in God.

33

While physical beauty and forms, which pollute you by their attachment, are passing away like syllables in their brief moments in God's song, you are tormented: the rust which has materialized is being scraped off.

Augustine, *De vera religione* 22; BA 8:80–82

34

Adversity says to you: 'You are trying to drive me away. You could certainly not stop me going, even if you wanted to—for I cannot remain when the Lord sings his song. I am only a syllable.'

35–6

(35) The good things of this world say: 'If God heals our corrupting disease, what will you do? Consider how you profit from us when you use us, and what you can thereby expect from us in the future. You know us by experience. So what? Do you want to be changed into us, or us to be changed into you? What have we to do with you? Why do you grieve at our passing away? We chose to perish in accordance with the Lord's will rather than remain in accordance with your yearnings. We bear you no gratitude for this love of yours: on the contrary, we deride it as folly. For whom above all must we obey—God or you? Say "me"—if you dare! Really, your only function is to turn us into refuse by consuming us. This is your usefulness, your power, that through you our needs can be abundantly met, for you cannot possibly make us last. Yet this is your endeavor, your happiness: not to be deprived of our contamination, to which you willingly succumb, while by means of it the Devil corrupts and defiles you, not without his own great delight and joy at your deception and ruin.

'O image of God, surely it is not thus that you resemble God? Surely this is not what God does? God is neither seduced nor compelled.'

(36) Furthermore, this world's goods say: 'Are you sure you use us of your own free will? Do we not draw you either to want something or not to want it? Is it not the case that I, coldness, a transient and insensate thing, force you to long for warmth? And others of us do the same. Consider whether you can really not want warmth when coldness presses upon you. Therefore you are our slave.'

Mt 8:29, Gen 1:26–27

37

If terrible and unmentionable corruption, experienced by the body, so delights and ravishes the soul, what will the highest good do?

38

Any experience arouses feelings, whether by attracting or by repelling us.

39

Even if you are sustained by transient goods, and at peace, you are still vulnerable to mice, lice, fleas and flies.

40

You desire peace for three years. Why not rather desire eternal peace, for years without end?

41

If your brother goes out of his mind and strikes you, you lose your temper: little mice can gnaw away at you, and you keep your temper, because they have no minds to lose.

42

To someone who has done you harm, be friendly and intimate —and apologetic and ashamed to someone you have harmed.

43

Just as you regard the good things people do for you as gifts of God and believe that all the thanks should go to him, so you should reckon the good things you do to people as God's good works, not yours. God lavishes his great gifts not for their own sake but for the sake of those on whom in his mercy he bestows them. It was by showing mercy to the gentiles that he glorified his apostles.

44

Just as chronic pains bring no more happiness than momentary ones do, so it is with taste and all the other things belonging to the bodily senses.

45

Anyone who bears a cross does not seek a long life, for he wants to lay it down quickly.

Lk 14:27

46

You are indulging in pleasures. You are therefore in a bad way. Why have doubts about withdrawing somewhere else, then, even to a life of austerity?

47

Why do you not rebuke in yourself what you blame in someone else, seeing that the same fault, or an even worse one, is in you?

48

You want to show off your self and to conceal your sin. So you do know how to distinguish between you and it!

49

God's creature is good: its defect, which is sin, is evil. It is as easy to distinguish between your brother and his fault, then, as it is between good and evil. Who, at the very sight of someone, gets angry or indignant with him? And who, on seeing the person's fault, does not take offense—apart from someone really wise and good who knows that the fault harms the person himself more than anyone else, and that therefore he is really to be pitied?

1 Tim 4:4

50

Nothing is more laborious for you than not to labor at all— in other words, to despise everything that gives rise to our labors, which means all that is subject to change.

Compare this text with Guigo's remark in the *Consuetudines Cartusiae* 14:5: 'For we regard nothing as more laborious in the exercises of monastic discipline than the silence and repose of solitude', SCh 313:196. Cf. also Augustine, *De vera religione* 35.65; BA 8:120: '. . . the friends of this world are so frightened of being separated from its embrace that nothing is more laborious for them than not to labor at all.'

51

To desire something as being good, in other words, as enjoyable and reliable, is one thing: it is another thing when something good is desired for someone else. Yet we find pleasure in both. One of them we owe to friends, the other to God alone. He alone ought to be desired as being good. When, therefore, this desire is directed to anyone but him, it is proof of flagrant idolatry.

52

When you love someone as a friend, yet desire wealth for him as something good, you love that infinitely more than him. You love him as someone in need, but the wealth as an end in itself, and so you are more ready to lose him than it.

53

How fair an art it is, to overcome evil with good! For opposites are conquered by each other.

Rom 12:21

54

Someone who strikes down a wicked man in his iniquity, because he hates iniquity and wants to see it destroyed, deceives himself: when a wicked man dies in his iniquity, his iniquity lasts for ever. So someone who hates iniquity must strive to correct the wicked man, and then iniquity itself will perish.

Ps 119 (118):163

55

If you should be like a lamb towards the most wicked people, what should you be like towards God, when he disciplines you with some chastisement?

Lk 10:3

56

The way to God is easy, for it is travelled by unburdening oneself. Yet it would be a hard way if it were travelled by means of burdening oneself. So, unburden yourself to the extent that, having left everything, you may deny your own self.

Lk 18:28, Mt 16:24

57

What God did not love in his friends and relatives—power, nobility, wealth, and honors—you are not to love in yours.

58

Your brother is filled with love and wisdom; and you do not share them. He is filled with anger, hatred and rage; and you cannot avoid sharing them. Someone who is insane needs sane people either to protect or to cure him.

59

You have been put here as an ensign to turn back the shafts of the enemy, that is, to destroy evil by opposing it with good. Yet you should never render evil for evil, except perhaps as medicine, in which case you are not rendering evil for evil, but good for evil.

Is 11:10, Lam 3:12, 1 Thess 5:15

60

What you eat, drink, wear, and sleep on are snares: everything is a snare.

Cf. Jerome, Ep 22.29: 'Remember that you walk in the midst of snares. . . .'; ed. Labourt, 1:143.

61

You are an exile by virtue of love, pleasure, and passion, not by virtue of where you are. You are an exile in the land of corruption, of the passions, of darkness, of ignorance, of evil loves and loathings.

62

Consider how many people like you will have striven for the world, and not only not obtained it, but lost themselves as well. But you, if you were to take the trouble, might win incomparably more than the object of all their labors, present and past.

Mk 8:34–36

63

If you take care of your flesh, your soul perishes too. But if you take care of your soul, both are saved.

64

It is the virtue of angels to live with vicious people and not to be corrupted by their vices. It is the virtue of the best doctors to live with the sick and mentally ill, and not only to avoid being corrupted in any way themselves, but also to restore them to health.

65

Those who love the world learn with great effort the art of obtaining and enjoying what they love. Now you want to obtain God, and yet do you not despise the very art by which he is won, that is, to render good for evil?

Ps 35(34):12

66

Either withdraw from this place, or do what you were put here for: that is, heal, and suffer.

67

Either place all your hope on these things, if you dare, and thus despise yourself; or abandon them altogether. Why are you hanging in suspense between the two? Why do you love or delight in what is difficult to obtain, impossible to keep, and what you dare not trust or love without anxiety?

68

The person who knows he is worthless accepts quietly and humbly the rebukes that come to him as his own opinions:

praises, however, he rejects as the opposite of his own opinions.

69

Consider that you are, in effect, at war. Thirst parches you, and you oppose it with drink: hunger tortures you, and you oppose it with food: cold, with clothes or a fire: disease, with medicine. Against all these you need patience and contempt of the world so as not to be overcome in another war which arises from them, in other words by hordes of vices.

70

Because all vices and sins exist for the sake of what is created—in other words, for the sake of the lowest of all good things—they bear witness to the goodness of the Creator, in other words, to the highest of all good things.

71

If the wind of favor of our human race, that is, reputation or praise, is so keenly sought, how much more should we seek the salvation of our human race, that is, the Creator?

72

If being called good is so delightful that even those who have no wish to be so—the wicked—rejoice at it, how much more delightful is it actually to be good? And if being called wicked is so bitter and horrible that even those who rejoice to do evil and exult in the very worst things cannot endure it, how much worse is it actually to be wicked?

Prov 2:14

73

People crave some created thing, and are fascinated by it, thereby forgetting themselves. When will you do the same with your Creator?

74

Think of all the things about you at which the devil can exclaim: 'Bravo, bravo!'

Ps 35(34):21, and Augustine, *Confessions* 1:13: 'I did not love you and went away from you in fornication, and in my fornication heard from all around me: "Bravo, bravo!"' CCSL 27:11–12; also Augustine, *Enarr. in Pss.* 69.8; CCSL 39: 938–9: 'Confound those who say to you: "Bravo, bravo!"'.

75

The Lord has summoned you to happiness—that is, to perfect love of him, from which comes an absence of trouble and fear—in other words, peace and security.

Jn 14:27

76

Since you are captivated only by pleasure, it is only against delectable things that you must be on your guard. Nowhere, then, is a Christian soul secure except in adversity.

77

This is our redemption: forgiveness of sins, enlightenment, being set aflame, eternal life. For us our God is all these things.

78

Transient things vex you. Why, then, do you not flee to other things—in other words, to the truth?

79

To the extent to which you love yourself—in other words, this present life—you must love the transient things without which you cannot exist. And to the extent to which you despise this life, you also despise the things that nourish it.

80

Do you regard anger as happiness? Isn't it really misery?

81

Sometimes evil simply causes displeasure, to no advantage whatever. It is as though two people, in one house, both want to have their own way, because of their pride. Each wants something evil. If their intentions cause mutual displeasure, this occurs not through their hatred of pride but through their love of it. The one who hates the other person's pride loves his own, which is obstructed by the other. This is a very hidden snare.

82

God has made rods for you out of the very things you love. Prosperity tortures you by eluding your grasp, tribulation by pressing upon you. Everything is a scourge, except God himself. And the one who destroys the scourge is like a child who breaks the rod of the father who beats it.

Prov 13:24

83

True love knows God.

1 Jn 4:7–8

84

The more noble and powerful a creature is, the more willingly it submits to the truth. Indeed it is powerful and noble precisely because of its submission.

85

It is stressful for you when you lose something or other, so you should not seek to lose things. Now the person who seeks to lose things is anyone who loves and acquires whatever cannot be kept.

86

No angry person is happy, or vice versa.

87

Insult any harlot you like—if you dare.

Jn 8:7

88

You must always reflect on what takes place within your own mind: not what others may do, whether they are good or bad, but what you can make of their deeds—in other words, how you can use their deeds, both good and bad, and how much you can profit from them, whether by favoring and helping them, or by having compassion and correcting them. For you draw what is good from all human actions when you are neither lured into favoring them by any of their good deeds, nor deterred from loving them by any of their wicked ones. When that happens, your love is disinterested. To be at peace with people is of no merit unless it be with those not at peace with us.

89

'God is love.' Whoever shows his love for someone else, other than for its own sake, sells both God and his own happiness too. A person's good comes only from loving.

1 Jn 4:8

90

If love and its telltale signs, a cheerful countenance and so on, please you so much in someone else, why are they not even more delightful in your own soul?

91

Those who are free have no need of someone to free them.

92

Look at the number of ways knowledge can make people suffer.

Si 1:18

93

The will of God for people, not people's will for God, is what must be done.

94

It is a good thing for you to be loved by holy people—indeed, it is to their immediate advantage too. By loving you, they experience the love that is God; and that very love becomes its own reward.

95

How does the truth treat you? With goodness. You should treat everyone in the same way.

96

Whom should we pity more, an innocent victim, or his murderer? The former lost the life of this world, which he ought to have despised of his own accord, while the latter lost the life that lasts for ever.

97

This person, who is your enemy, is a fool: that one, who is the devil, is crafty, because he uses the first one to attack you. With the former, be agreeable, so you can free him: against the latter, be on your guard.

98

What profits you most? The truth. It is demonstrably above all other things because it delights the best of angels and human beings alike.

99

Are hazelnuts and blackberries inherently appetizing, while truth and peace are not?

Zech 8:19

100

Because a defect, a weakness, a craving, and a sorrow each demand something to assuage them, sheer habit arranges it.

They demand what you are in the habit of giving them: they are 'leaning on their beloved'.

Song of Songs 8:5

101

The Lord did not ask his enemies to set him free, but his Father, for 'there is no power except from God'.

Rom 13:1

102

So long as your spirit is not moved by anger, hatred, sorrow, fear, or by what causes these things, nothing that happens to you now will do you any harm in the life to come.

103

All misery consists in this: that everybody loves one thing above all else, on which they unwaveringly set their hearts. What is it for you?

104

Notice how all people, as though having discovered treasure, grab a piece of the world and fasten their attention on their own particular piece, or indeed are torn between many different pieces: just as a dog, set between two pieces of meat, does not know which he should go for first, for fear of losing the other one.

105

All people think they are living life well. Each one, fully persuaded in his own mind, either thinks he is doing what is good for him, or bemoans the fact that he isn't. And furthermore, the one who bemoans thinks that this does him good. All of them are mistaken.

Rom 14:5

106

Happy is the person who chooses a secure place for his work. Now this is what a secure choice and worthwhile work consists of: the desire to do good to all, reflecting the fact that you want them to be people who do not need your help. For the more concerned people seem to be with their own interests, the less good they are doing. For the distinctive good of each individual consists in the desire to do good to all. But who understands this? Anyone who seeks to work for his own good, therefore, not only finds nothing good but also does great harm to his soul. While he is seeking his own good, which cannot exist anyway, he is turned away from the common good, that is, from God. For just as there is one nature common to all human beings, so also there is one common good.

107

When someone speaks evil of you, and it is not true, he harms himself, not you. He is deceiving himself. It is as if he were to call gold dung: what harm would that do to the gold? Yet if the evil which is said of you is true, you are being taught what to guard against.

Someone who praises something good benefits himself, not the person he is praising. So when someone tells you something good about yourself, are you not in effect being told idle reports concerning something that you know more about than anyone? Criticize no one but yourself.

108

If people want you to pray for someone, they say to you: 'He is so holy, so good!' It is as though a sick man were brought

to the doctor, who is told: 'Heal him, cure him, because he's
so healthy.' Or is this said so that you may thereby begin to
hope for his salvation?

People also say: 'Pray for him, because he has done you
good'. But you should rather do this because he has done you
wrong, for then he needs it. 'They that are whole need not a
physician, but they that are sick.' And by doing that you will
be a child of God.

Lk 5:31, Mt 5:9

109

A senseless spiritual turmoil—that is what misery is. It almost
always occurs in you when God in his mercy destroys what
causes you to die—in other words, those things to which you
were wrongly attached—so that, by abandoning them, you
may live.

110

Why do you snatch for yourself what displeases you in someone else—in other words, anger? For that means that you
are angry because the other person is! You should instead be
angry with yourself precisely because you are angry. If anger
itself really displeased you, you would not find room for it,
but flee from it. That only happens by keeping the peace.

111

Sometimes anger so displeases you that you rush headlong
into hatred. If someone else's anger displeases you, let your
own hatred do the same.

112

When someone calls you just, you are in a way being criticized, as if gilded wood were put on display as something
precious. It would not be gilded if it shone enough by itself.

113

A lake should not pride itself on being full of water: that comes from its source. So it should be with you with regard to peace. Something else is always the cause of your peace; and the more unstable the source of your peace, the more frail and fickle that peace is. How little value it has, then, when its source is the charm of a human face!

114

Everyone deeply longs to be secure. The more he can be unsettled, the less secure he is. Yet the more the things he loves are susceptible of becoming something different from what he wants, the more he can be unsettled. So, let anyone at all say to you: 'I am going to do you harm; I am going to take away your peace of mind—in fact I shall think, or may even speak, evil about you.' And see how susceptible he is of being upset and disturbed—to the same extent as your own peace of mind is shattered and dispelled.

The translation follows mss M,T,B and P.

115

Spiritual turmoil is what misery is. Now this almost always occurs in you when the Lord in his mercy takes from you the swords by which your enemy was destroying you—that is, good things which are subject to change, and to which you were wrongly attached.

116

If you rely on a full cellar, aren't you behaving like money-lenders? And is that not to worship an idol, even though a cellar has no face or eyes? In any case, you do not realize how much you rely on a full cellar until it is empty.

117

Someone who gives something to another because the other person is either giving or about to give something in return, receives no thanks from God. This is what you are doing with regard to peace and love.

118

Delightful things are to be avoided when we want to find peace from our cravings or other passions, in case the very pleasure we experience in them make us begin to love precisely the emotional turmoil they cause.

119

You reproach the doctor when you despair of the patient. For the ease with which the one is healed is commensurate with the ability and loving concern of the one who is healing him.

120

Only truth knows how to depart from evil, and only love of truth is able to do so. You do not depart from evil by moving from one place to another.

Ps 37(36):27

121

If the things you rely on or take delight in were to do the same with regard to themselves, you would deride them as ridiculous—indeed you would grieve for them as lost. And if everyone is crazy in this way, is it good for you to be crazy too?

122

If you put up with yourself as an unclean person, why not with everyone else?

123

Your spirit is subject to as many hazards as are the things you love.

124

First of all, driven by physical suffering, you allowed the world in. But now you take delight in suffering precisely so that you can experience and enjoy the world.

125

Truth is more bitter to us than any adversity, because each adversity strikes at just one or several pleasures, whereas the truth condemns all of them at once. Now if you experienced all the colors and other things perceptible through the eyes and other physical senses, and if you either recounted or simply listened to all the gossip that is around, what good would it do you? This is so no matter how important the things you have experienced or heard about.

Cf. Jerome, Ep 40.1: "Nature regards truth as bitter while vices are seen as agreeable" (ed. Labourt 2:85)

126

What good would a doctor be if there were no diseases? What need would there be of people who were strong and persevering if there were no adversities? If there were no guilt, what would be the use of intercessors? If there were no fools, what use would teachers be? If there were no one who suffered want, what need of helpers?

And you, would you heal if there were none to heal, no sick people? Would you suffer if there were nothing to endure, no adversities? Would you intercede if there were none to pray for, none who were guilty? Would you teach if there were none to instruct, no fools? Would you help others if there were none who needed it, no one who suffered want?

You have things back to front! And what else? Would you eat, if there were no hunger? Would you drink, if there were no thirst? Would you warm yourself, if there were no cold? Would you look for shade, if there were no heat? Everything is the wrong way round.

127

You cannot hate anyone without acknowledging your own wickedness. To want good things even for the wicked is a characteristic of saints.

128

You should love truth alone, and the peace that flows from it.

Zech 8:19

129

It is the mark of greatness to intercede for those who confess, so that they may be forgiven. The mark of those who are greater still is to pray in love even for those who do not yet recognize their guilt, so that they may become aware of it; and also for those who do not confess it, either because they are ashamed or because they love their guilt, so that they may confess it.

130

The closer you are to love of this life, and to all that goes with it, the closer you are to wickedness.

131

If you take away all these bandages—clothes and the like—you will see whether you are really healthy.

132

Happiness must be capable of perception or understanding, so that someone who becomes happy can give thanks to it for its own sake. Who would take the trouble to thank or please something that did not understand?

133

O you who are choosing a spiritual father or doctor, let me give you this advice: choose someone whose spirit will not be distracted from you, by illness or anything else.

134

The one thing you want God to show you—kindness—you must show everyone, either by discipline or by gentleness.

135

Why do you insult the blind and infirm when you are like them—or, if you are different, when it is not through your doing or to your credit?

136

Consider what you should do if everyone were always driven by anger and folly. Should you be disturbed on that account? Then why, when just one person is sometimes disturbed, are you disturbed too? You ought to give him medicine, not further disturbance. How can folly be cured by someone acting foolishly?

137

One kind of peace is found in someone who has completely overcome adversity, and another in someone who flees or thinks he has fled from it. You rejoice, not because you have

either overcome or avoided adversity, but because you have
been overcome by it, or soon will be.

138

'I came not to judge the world, but to save it'—in other words,
I did not come to execute upon the guilty the sentence of condemnation they deserved, but to show them with compassion
how they can avoid it.

Jn 12:47

139

Why does the suffering of your fellow human beings please
you? Because it is just? In that case, your own suffering should
please God, because it is just. But such an opinion consigns
you to everlasting fire. If someone who kills a chicken is
judged worthy of death, to what punishment would someone
who kills a human being be subjected?

140

Reprove or chastise someone only if you love him, if you are
impelled by love itself. If you do it from any other motive,
you condemn yourself. Therefore act towards others in the
spirit in which you want God to do all things to you.

Mt 7:12

141

Do not let transient things be the source of your peace, for
then it will be as worthless and fragile as they are. That kind
of peace you have in common with beasts: let yours be the
peace you have in common with angels—in other words, the
kind that proceeds from truth.

142

Do not drive people away, but drive away from them what rightly offends you—that is to say, vice. And do this out of love for them—just as you want for yourself. It is not human nature that offends you, but the vices which impair it. Why probe the bleeding wounds of your own race, unless it is to heal them—as you should your own?

You should be concerned not with what others do, but with what you do. For the person who is of value to all is the one who pays attention not so much to what others do as to what he makes of them and their deeds, whether good or evil. You can bring good from both, but much more particularly and notably from evil.

If you are going to reject evil people, begin with yourself. The good and the evil are raw material from which a just person can bring profit—rejoicing with the former, and having compassion on the latter.

143

The body, being at the mercy of stronger forces, is either driven or seduced. So too the will. But you should concern yourself with what can overcome and move, not the body, but the mind and will.

144

Do everything for the sake of peace, the route towards which lies through truth alone, which is your adversary in this journey. Thus you must either subject it to you, or yourself to it: no other option is open to you.

Mt 5:25

145

For the sake of peace and happiness, despise everything you have held onto and loved, unless you want to lose peace and happiness altogether.

146

You grumble because you are not being obeyed. O shame, what has become of you? Did God create human beings to be subject and obedient to you, rather than to himself, to God?

147

You are disturbed because I am. One disturbed person finds fault with another. O shame! 'Let the one who stands upright deride the bandy-legged, the white man laugh at the Ethiopian.' Let me be corrected, and do this wicked thing no longer. But what about you? What will you do about this vice of yours? Not only are you unable to cure me of it: you cannot even cope with it yourself.

Juvenal, *Satires* 2:23

148

You dishonourably love a maidservant, in other words a creature. Only because of that do you suffer agonies when her master—that is, your God—deals with her according to his good pleasure.

149

You lingered on one of the notes of a great song: as a result you are upset when the singer in his infinite wisdom continues the song. The one note that you loved is taken away from you, and others follow it in their due order, since he is not singing just for you, nor at your bidding, but at his own. The notes that follow are uncongenial to you, because they take the place of the one you wrongly loved.

150

Your natural place is to be a good companion and friend of people, not their proud master. Do everything, therefore, with companionable love, not with overbearing arrogance.

151

Love must be drunk for its own sake, because of its own sweetness, like the most delicious nectar. Even if everyone were to go crazy, it is not to be sold at any price. For love does us good, and makes us happy, whatever others may do.

152

A person who loves something that should not be loved is miserable and foolish, even if neither he nor it should perish. Is an idolater miserable only because the thing he worships is perishable? In that case, he would not be miserable if it did not perish. Certainly, for as long as his idol remains, he is its most wretched worshipper, even if sound in body and rich in this world's goods.

153

Adversities do not make you miserable; but they disclose to you and teach you that you were already.

154

Worldly successes darken the mind by concealing and increasing wretchedness, not by taking it away.

155

One might reasonably, and without fear of contradiction, say 'snow is white', because it is true. It is no less true that someone who says 'snow is black' is lying. One might therefore say, just as reasonably and incontestably: 'If you accept this because it is true, from now on you are not to oppose anything that is true'. For if this apple pleases you because it is sweet, why doesn't everything with the same taste please you just as much?

156

You want to live in this world like a riotous and depraved son in the home of a good father. You want God and his works to yield to your depraved will and to serve it, not you to do the same to God's.

Lk 15:11–32

157

You should want no change of any kind for yourself, except of yourself, in other words a change in your own knowledge and will. If you must seek changes in other things, you should do so only for their own sakes. Even the evil deeds of other people can be of value to you, if you respond to them as you should.

158

Assess the nature of someone's opinion or preference, of praise as well as blame, just as you assess the nature of roots and any such things.

159

The love of each belongs to all, for each person should love everyone. So someone who wants this love to be shown to him in particular is a thief, and thereby makes himself an offender against everyone.

160

If someone has a wound lanced or cauterized, he cries out— and no wonder, for he is in pain. So it is with someone who is rebuked. But why are you, who are doing this, moved unless it is purely out of compassion for him?

161

If it is a good thing to be affected by transient things, then it must be good actually to be these things. But do not envy any of them: you are better than them all.

162

The beginning of the return to the truth is dissatisfaction with yourself for your falsehood.

Cf. Augustine, *De vera religione* 39:72: 'Return into yourself: for truth dwells in the interior person', BA 8:130.

163

A servant of the truth should love what he serves, and whom he serves. And when that very thing is served to him by someone else, he should receive it with gratitude, as something that he loves.

164

Let love be your motive for speaking the truth, as it would be for an act of healing. If someone does not accept it, then you either pity him, or refuse to love him, or regard what he is rejecting as worthless. It would be like a sick man spitting out wholesome medicine.

165

Truth leads to eternal peace, which we have in common with the angels. Falsehood leads to labor and sorrow, which we have in common with the devil.

Ps 90(89):10

166

In the last analysis, no one will ever regret having thought that gold is gold, or earth is earth, because it is true. But we

regret with some difficulty having regarded as worth loving
something that isn't, or having put our hopes in something
we shouldn't, because they are not to be loved or hoped for.
Yet someone who thinks that one should love what shouldn't
be loved is just as wrong as someone who thinks that what is
not gold is gold. The first of these is deadly, while the second,
though certainly an error, is not really very harmful. And yet
how many people are afraid of the latter error, and how few
the former!

167

Notice how you can love the harvest in anticipation in the
young shoot, and the twisted stem. In the same way, love
those who are not yet good.

Cf. Augustine, *Confessions* 3.9 (CCSL 27:36): 'But amongst these vices . . .
are the sins into which men fall although they are in general on the right
way. By those who judge rightly, these sins are blamed according to the
rule of perfection, but the persons themselves may still be praised for the
hope of a better harvest, as the blade gives hope of the growing corn' trans.
F. J. Sheed (London, 1941) p. 41.

168

Treat everyone just as the truth has treated you. Just as it
supported and loved you with a view to making you better,
so you must support and love others to make them better.

169

If in a court case your cause is just, let justice alone suffice for
you. Do not look for someone to take your side unless it is to
persuade him or your opponents, as people you love, to make
that same justice their own. A person who judges justly serves
the interests of those who obtained things unjustly, because
he leads them back to justice.

170

Someone who espouses the cause of justice benefits himself, not it. After all, justice is not something that needs defending; but we need to flee to it for protection—otherwise we shall perish. However, the highest form of justice consists in not defending oneself.

171

Give me, if you can, a love or a fear that has no object. If you are fascinated by something, you set it aside only with reluctance. Ignorance is the mother of admiration, and so is novelty.

This meditation consists of three explicit allusions to earlier writers. The first sentence alludes to Augustine, *Enarrationes in Psalmos* 31.2; the second to Horace, *Epistolae* 1.10; the third to Augustine, *Confessions* 13.21.

172

Someone wanting to hurt you should arm himself with your life, in other words with the truth. Truth is the life of your soul. Thus your own life wounds you, because you protect yourself with falsehood.

173

People use the truth like a sword, in itself a good thing; but they use it to do harm, because they have an evil intent, and actually inflict evil with it. Do not yourself use it in this way, but rather with the intention of doing good to the person for whom you wield it. Great would be the injury done to you by someone who considered you so wicked and malicious that, when he wanted to avenge himself on some enemy of his, he handed you over to him, or even inflicted you on him as a punishment.

174

Your joy in possessing great wisdom must not exceed your fear of misusing it.

175

You must not be an arrogant master of people, but a good companion. You must delight, not in their multiple pleasures, but in their simple good, in other words in the truth.

176

Consider what a gulf there is between the five senses on the one hand, and faith and understanding on the other.

177

In all the care which you take for your own salvation, you have no more profitable service or remedy than to reproach and despise yourself. So anyone who does this for you is your helper. He is doing what you were doing, or should have been doing, to set forward your salvation.

178

Like knowledge, feelings in effect pass from one person to another. If a person 'puts nothing into your mouth'—in other words, if he does not do what pleases you—you 'proclaim a holy war on him'. In this text, take 'mouth' to mean 'will'.

Micah 3:5. The translation follows *The New English Bible*.

179

Peace is the blessing of the spirit in which it dwells. Thus you are to set your heart on it for its own sake, like a sweet savor.

Let it be so strong in you that you do not exclude even the wicked from it.

180

Adversities do not make you worse than you are, but they do show you how much worse you have become. You grew worse when you became attached to the things which adversities destroy. Indeed you were already blind or sick when you were attached to them. Your attachment stems from your distorted attitude of mind.

181

Like a note in a song, everything in the world's course has its place in space or time. You are suffering because you became attached to inferior things which pass away when their turn comes.

182

If you love because you are loved, or so that you will be loved, you are not really loving but reciprocating, repaying love for love. You are a moneychanger! You have had your reward.

Mt 6:2

183

If there were no language, would God not speak to human beings perfectly well through the adversities they suffer—in themselves or in their love of external things—and even through their prosperity?

184

All the things which we call adversities are only adversities for the wicked—in other words, for those who love the creature in place of the Creator.

185

Whenever you change anything, you do it either so that it ceases to exist or so that it improves. Each action is preceded either by criticism or by disapproval. You should employ the first of these with regard to people, the second with regard to their vices.

186

Love what you can never lack when you love it: in other words, God.

187

Consider how much light and strength you possess, so much that you cannot be seduced or constrained; and in this alone is freedom. Consider too how quickly you can be seduced or constrained, since you are so blind and weak. Insofar as you can be constrained at all, however, you have already been seduced. The question is not whether that is pleasant, but whether you should love it, or depend on it. By what sure arguments or scriptural texts, by what precepts and examples, by what sacraments can you prepare and strengthen yourself to act responsibly in this regard? You know how to tell whether some object is made of gold. But how do you tell whether you should love it, or depend on it? It is one thing to be gold, but quite another to be worthy of love. Gold, after all, is just gold, whereas something worthy of love is not just gold—indeed, it is not gold at all.

188

Consider how the soul is captivated by physical things, and, once captivated, is tormented, just like a child who is captivated the moment he sees a sparrow. Once he gets hold of it, he is exposed to as many hazards as the sparrow itself. Think how safe the soul is before it is captivated by things like that. The things that give it pleasure hold it in their power, causing it to be afflicted by adversity.

The argument of this Meditation is developed in Meditation 454.

189

A foolish doctor who does not want his reputation to suffer blames his patients for anything that does not turn out well, even though the fault is his. This is what you do with those under your authority.

190

Seek to be taught, rather than to teach. This is the approach of anyone who knows himself well. In the same way you should seek to be helped and protected.

191

Your burden is light in comparison with the Lord's; and even that you do not bear as you should.

192

Whatever you read in books you can see with your own eyes in people—in other words, what you must avoid, and what you must do.

193

The way you would feel about all people if you were far away from them, and reflecting on their sins and miseries, must be the way you feel about them now, when with your own eyes you see them perishing through blindness or weakness. The devil is either deceiving or overcoming them through things that are transient.

194

Wanting the things you consume, such as food and clothing, to be elegant, is like wanting to have firewood painted. You need clothes because of the cold, not because they are this or that color; and you need food because you are hungry, not because it has this or that taste.

Si 11:4

195

The aim of a good teacher or doctor is twofold: to preserve and increase the good already present—in other words, health or knowledge; to supply what is lacking, and to remove what is evil. For 'drunkenness besets the thirsty person'. But someone who wants things to remain thus is not a good teacher or doctor. Someone who wants always to be a doctor wants there always to be sick people; and someone who wants always to be a teacher wants ignorant people. He hates those he wants always to be in that condition. But someone who is good fights against disease and ignorance in order to destroy them. He is, in a sense, fighting against his own profession, in order to destroy it: if those evils were no longer to exist, neither would his job.

Deut 29:19

196

Consider how the Lord chides you whenever you reach out covetously beyond him towards created things—just as a nurse smacks a child's arm when it is stretched out beyond his cradle, in case he dies of cold.

197

Since you don't want to be deceived about anything, why do you let it happen when it comes to happiness, or reward?

198

Nothing must be done for its own sake, other than knowing and loving God.

199

Consider how everything is sought, either for its own sake or for the sake of something else. To put it another way, each thing is either striven for in its own right, or it is striven for as a means to an end, such as cows and everything else you possess or do—even the way you use bread.

200

Your reward will depend not on the progress of those entrusted to your charge, but on your motive and effort, whether they make progress or not. For never, ever, does integrity increase with success.

The last sentence derives from Lucan, *Pharsalia* (*De bello civili*), 9.571.

201

Everyone tries to achieve what he or she wants, as if all of them were certain that what they want is good. But remind them all of this: that they should try to want what is right for them.

202

Someone who praises you for your holiness aspires to higher things. What pleases him is above you—in other words, holiness. If you love him as someone who is pleased not by holiness but by you, then you aspire to lower things.

203

An animal's pleasure comes from the bodily senses: the devil's from every kind of pride, and from jealousy and deceit. A philosopher's pleasure comes from knowledge of created things: an angel's from knowing and loving God.

204

The truth is not to be defended: it defends others. Truth does not need you: you need it.

205

'Let not your heart be troubled, neither let it be afraid'—this is the true Sabbath, celebrated by someone who is neither seduced nor constrained by others, but is self-possessed. He can turn himself into a gift for others, allowing himself to be either angry or calm, depending on which he judges profitable for them.

Jn 14:27

206

If this or that person were to work as hard for God as he works for the world, his anniversary would be celebrated like that of a martyr.

207

Just as cold comes from ice, so a useless fear comes from love of transient things: this fear, together with other kinds of misery, invades the soul. Which kind of misery is worse—cold, or this useless fear? Isn't it fear?

So put away from yourself everything that causes this fear, just as you do with what causes cold, by which I mean that you must remove it not from wherever you happen to be, but from your soul. You should fear only what can and should be avoided—in other words, sin. Whatever you ought to avoid, that is to say iniquity, you can avoid, with God's help.

208

Consider how much you are in the power of other people and capable of being disturbed and tormented by them. Just as it is easy for them to abuse you verbally, or in their thoughts, so it is easy for you to be disturbed. What would you do, then, if they wanted to strike you? If you annoy them, you become disturbed yourself, which means that you are in their power. And whether this happens or not, you are still vulnerable because of your state of mind. If you annoy them when you are doing good, this harms them, not you, so endeavor to change their hearts, not the good you are doing. If you annoy them when you are doing evil, what harms you is not causing annoyance in itself—in fact that does you good—but your evil deeds.

209

'The love of God has been shed abroad in our hearts through the Holy Spirit which is given to us.' But you love neither God nor your neighbor except for the sake of temporal benefit. It is through temporal things, then, that love is shed abroad in you, not through the Holy Spirit. In that case it is not love that is shed abroad, but covetousness.

Rom 5:5

210

When you rebuke someone, you could not possibly be doing him more good. However, you will not be reckoned to have done well unless you do this for his good, in other words out of the love in which you hold him dear.

211

The truth is too bitter and unpleasant for people; and that is not its fault, but theirs, for it is like a bright light to weak eyes.

Take care, then, not to make it even more bitter by failing to speak it as you should, out of love.

For it is out of love that a devoted doctor, administering a wholesome but bitter medicine, smears the edge of the cup with honey. In this way, while what is sweet is taken readily, what is wholesome is swallowed in the same easy gulp. Your entire duty is to do good to all.

212

Every rational soul that wants to take revenge on someone inflicts on another something that it fears and hates and regards as evil for itself. But when it wants to do this, there is nothing it seizes upon more readily than the truth, and no evil that it inflicts with more venomous intention. Consequently there is nothing that it hates more for itself than to hear the truth spoken. Certainly, what is said by one enemy to another can win eternal salvation, if the one to whom it is said accepts it humbly. Someone who calls an adulterer an adulterer says to him out of malice what he ought to admit freely for the sake of his own salvation. He should accept this readily, paying attention not to the motive from which it is spoken, but to what is actually said to him.

213

If you speak the truth, not through love of the truth, but through a desire to hurt someone, you will receive not the reward of one who speaks the truth, but the punishment of one who slanders.

214

The very thing you inflict on other people out of malice you would yourself regard as malicious if someone were to inflict it on you, and vice versa.

215

If someone to whom you say a word about some aspect of his wickedness suffers so much as a result, consider how much distress you will suffer when the true light reveals you completely to yourself. For then the counsels of the hearts will be made manifest.

1 Cor 4:5

216

Whether you find fault with someone else, or someone else finds fault with you, you are equally to blame. In each case you are either receiving or inflicting the truth as though it were something evil. Thus someone who wants to scourge you may seize hold of your life—in other words, the truth—so as to beat and torment you with it.

217

The martyrs say to God: 'For your sake we are put to death all the day long'. You are to say to any worthless trifles: 'For your sakes I am troubled all the day long'.

Ps 44(43):22

218

Hold yourself in check and gather your wits about you—if you don't, you will lay yourself open to all that is fleeting in transient things; and that will cause you torment.

219

Notice that your task is no different from what it was before you became prior. Then you were accomplishing by your wishes, prayers and desires what now you have begun to accomplish by actions, which is to do good to all. The things

you do should not diminish your desires, but enlarge them
with new vigor.

220

If you should render evil to those who have sinned—and to do
this is your salvation—then devote yourself wholeheartedly to
this task. So start with yourself: there is no one of whose sin
you can be more certain. Then set about everyone else, for
'all have sinned'. Carry out this task as far as you can; and
desire to do it even when you cannot. It is enough to desire
the good that you cannot accomplish; but a person who does
not at least desire the good that he cannot accomplish is guilty
indeed.

Rom 3:23

221

Once, when an ants' nest was destroyed, you saw how anx-
iously each one seized what it loved—in other words, an egg—
heedless of its own safety. It is in this manner that you must
love truth and peace—in other words, God.

Zech 8:19

222

The more highly a person prizes this world's goods, the more
he grieves when he is without them, and suffers with others
who are without them too. The less he values them, the less
he minds when he or others lack them. So it is with eternal
things: therefore the greatest of all are those people who have
compassion on errors and sins.

223

Let others have compassion on people's bodies: you must have
compassion on their spirits.

224

There could be no way back to salvation for the publican except by humbly confessing his sins, for which the Pharisee was arrogantly taunting him.

Lk 18:9–14

225

Truth is life, and eternal salvation. You should therefore have compassion on someone who is displeased by it, for insofar as this is the case, he is dead and utterly lost. But you, perverse person that you are, would not speak the truth to him unless you thought it would be bitter and unbearable to him; for you judge others by your own standards. Yet the worst thing of all is the way in which, to please others, you speak the truth, which they love or admire, as if you were uttering lies or flattery.

Look at wormwood, which is both bitter and healthy for someone you care about. You give it to him not because it is bitter, but because it is healthy: the former action is cruel, the latter kind.

So the truth is to be spoken neither because it displeases nor because it pleases someone, but so it may do him good. You should refrain from speaking it only if it would harm someone, like light for weak eyes.

226

Alas for those who have lost, not transient things, but the spirit of endurance! No suffering is overcome except by that. You do not dispose of hunger by eating—you serve its interests, just as you serve thirst by drinking. These actions tend to incline the soul to delight in the external forms of bodies; and when that happens, these things are not overcome, but rule over us by achieving their aim, which is to make our spirit submit, and to lay the groundwork for yet easier and greater submission.

227

You deplored your body's lack of stature: you did not deplore your spirit's lack of strength to take it in good heart.

228

Which of these do you rejoice more at obtaining, or grieve more at losing—something that is better than other things, or something that is loved more? Something that is loved more, irrespective of whether it is better or worse. But what is loved more? Something regarded as being better. And what is regarded as being better? The thing that gives the greater pleasure.

This is false. For it is not in proportion to the true value of things that we grieve at their loss or rejoice at their gain, but in proportion to the love which subjects us to them. Indeed, of two things, we grieve more at the loss, or rejoice more at the gain, of the one we love more, irrespective of whether it is worse or better. This is utterly perverse. A person will grieve even at losing an egg, and yet not at losing God, who is the highest good of all.

229

Everything a person does is done out of a desire for things to go well for himself, or at any rate not to go badly. And how sad it is always to be striving for happiness, or for the avoidance of evil, by means of something that not only fails to attain it but invariably drives it further away—in other words, by means of vice. How sad it is that a divinely given exertion and will by means of which a person may strive for and attain happiness is entirely devoted to immersing that person in misery—in other words, to enjoying things that will perish.

230

Each person should flee from his own vices: those of others will do him no harm.

231

Concern for others' sins is a vice; and so is a lack of it. But both become virtues, if you add to them a desire to correct. Take away love, and vice is all that remains.

232

What you are to strive for is not that people should be unable to sin, but that they should not want to. What is laudable is not being unable to sin, but being unwilling to do so. If wanting to sin is already a sin, no one can restrain people from sinning except someone who can stop their wanting to sin—in other words, God alone. If only we could not want to sin, for then we could not do so!

233

It is powerful impotence to be unable to want what is evil. The reason why the Lord is all-powerful is because he cannot want what is evil. To be able to want what is harmful for you is at once an impotent and mighty power; and the more you want it, the weaker you will be, and the more subject to your enemies.

Cf. Augustine, *De correptione et gratia* 12.33: 'the first freewill (i.e. of the first human being) consisted in being able not to sin; the last will be much greater—not being able to sin.' PL 44:936

234

Among all the works of man, the greatest is to want what he ought to want. The more a person wants this, the more he attains it; and the more he attains it, the more he wants it—to desire what is really good is in fact to attain it. But what is really good? Justice. And what is really evil? Wickedness.

235

We share the joy or the pain of those we consider happy or miserable. Now we consider happy or miserable those people whom we see either enjoying, or doing without, those things which we regard as good and worth loving. So, in the case of transitory things, someone who shares either the joy of those who delight in them, or the pain of those who lack them, is certainly free from jealousy; but he is nevertheless regarding as worth loving goods which will perish.

236

Christ's name is Jesus. So from the moment that, for whatever reason, you lose the desire to save anyone at all, you cut yourself off from the members of Christ—in other words, from the savior.

'Jesus' means 'the one who saves'; see Mt 1:21.

237

Why do you want to send that brother away? Because he is full of anger and every possible vice. Then may God do the same to you. Your own words demonstrate precisely why you should not send him away. 'They that are whole need not a physician, but they that are sick.' If you were to ask a mother why she is abandoning her son, and she answers: 'Because he is weak and ill', you would have to ask her if she would like her son to do the same to her. And if she were to answer: 'No', you would have to add: 'Then your reason for hating him is a bad one'. The same thing applies to a physician.

Mt 9:12

238

Prayer, instruction*, and example—these are the things we long to be granted by the saints; and we should, with diligence and conscientiousness, grant them to others. To be unwilling to do good is actually to do harm, since the Lord says 'Love your neighbor as yourself'. So it is, then, that all belong to each, and each to all. Therefore someone who does not love me steals from me what God has given me, by taking away his love from me.

doctrina—teaching or instruction, as in the Rule of Saint Benedict, Prol. 50; see Adalbert de Vogüé, *The Rule of Saint Benedict: A Doctrinal and Spiritual Commentary*, CS 54 (Kalamazoo, 1983) 26.

Mt 19:19

239

We love one thing, such as God, because we need it, so that by means of it we may become good or happy: we love another, such as other people, because we are good, and not because we need it. We love others because we wish them well. Nevertheless, a person is not entirely good or happy if he is not good to others. Misery born of separation from God and love for this fleeting song that is the world is what makes us bad to others.

240

Among transitory things, the most delightful are the most deadly.

241

What wife is impudent enough to say to her husband: 'Find me so-and-so for me to sleep with: he attracts me more than you. Otherwise I won't be able to rest'? Yet this is the way you treat your husband—in other words, the Lord—when, by loving something else more than him, you ask that very thing from him.

242

You abandoned your husband—in other words, God—and attached yourself to his slave, the world. Whatever evil befalls you, either from it or on its account, there will be no one to whom you may presume to cry for help.

243

When you say to God, 'Give me this or that', what you are really saying is, 'Give me something with which I can offend you, and commit fornication against you.' When you ask him for anything other than himself, you reveal your guilt and your fornication to him by the very fact of your request, and you do not realize it.

Hos 9:1, Ps 73(72):27, Augustine, *Confessions* 1.13; CCSL 27:11

244

It is just as stupid, if not more so, to bend the knee before things you may have made yourself, as it is to submit your spirit to things you do away with—in other words, to flavors and other objects of the senses.

245

Consider how, as if you were in a tavern, you have sold your love like a prostitute: you weigh it out, just as you would perishable gifts, to people whose physical forms will perish; and you have even sold it for nothing. In this tavern no one receives anything if he does not give something, or is at least expected to give something. And yet you would have nothing to sell if it had not been given you freely from above. You have had your reward, then: you have built your house as a moth does, laying an unstable foundation that is certain to collapse.

Jn 19:11, Mt 6:2, Job 27:18

246

Tremble before the inscrutable judgments of God upon you. For whatever authority you have over others, you have no idea why they did not have the same authority over you. Therefore, behave towards them as you think they ought to have behaved towards you, if they had been in your position.

247

It is one thing to want to harm someone, another to want to correct him. The former springs from cruelty, the latter from love.

248

You should be angry with a sinner, but only if you believe it will do him good.

249

Whatever form you delight in has the same effect on your mind as a man has on a woman. Your mind yields and succumbs to it, rather than the other way round: you are conformed and assimilated to it. The image of this form remains imprinted on your mind, like a statue in its temple, to which you sacrifice, not a bullock or a goat, but your rational soul and body—in other words, your entire self—whenever you delight in it.

Ps 66(65):15

250

Those who seek forgiveness for themselves should not exact vengeance from others.

251

Bread—in other words, the truth—strengthens the human heart, so that it does not succumb to physical forms.

Ps 104(103):15

252

The love of a transient peace necessarily gives birth to a restless mind. Whoever possesses this kind of peace, and loves it, necessarily lacks true peace.

253

When you have clearly proved someone to be a criminal, you will have to weep over his sin, since the Lord wept over yours. Why do you pry into the sickness of an invalid if, after diagnosing it, you not only refuse him sympathy or remedies, but offer him insults as well?

254

When you suffer in any way, whether through fear, anger, hatred, or any kind of grief, you should blame only yourself for it—your cravings, ignorance and laziness. If someone wants to hurt you, blame that on his cravings. Your injury and grief bear witness to your sin, for by abandoning God you have plainly fallen in love with something that can harm you.

255

Alas for the person whose happiness or pleasure has an end and a beginning!

256

'Letting the ship give way to the wind, we were driven by

it'—towards either joy or grief, depending on the alternation of whatever forms presented themselves.

Acts 27:15

257

'He has gathered them out of all the lands.' In other words: rescuing the faithful from tastes and perfumes and carnal contacts, he has gathered them to himself.

Ps 107(106):2

258

In any situation where you are able to maintain chastity with regard to God, you are also able to maintain justice with regard to your neighbor. This is done by not yielding to your cravings.

259

If you do not look askance on those who do you evil, you will be at peace with them.

Ps 37(36):1

260

The way you behave in this world suggests that you only came here to stare and wonder at physical forms.

261

It is one thing to know what sin is by experiencing and committing it: it is another to know it by discerning and denouncing it. The latter is the work of the just person, the former of the wicked.

262

Let others journey to Jerusalem: you should journey to humility or patience. The latter means that you travel beyond the world, the former only within it.

Cf. Jerome, Ep. 58.3: 'Both from Jerusalem and from Britain the heavenly hall lies equally open; for the kingdom of God is within you. Antony, and the hosts of monks in Egypt and Mesopotamia, Pontus, Cappadocia and Armenia have not seen Jerusalem; and the gate of paradise lies open for them far away from that city.' (ed. Labourt 3:77). Like Saint Bernard (Ep. 64.1, ed. Leclercq 7:157), Guigo preferred monks to seek the heavenly Jerusalem rather than to join the crusaders. For this characteristic monastic emphasis on seeking an 'interior' Jerusalem, see Giles Constable, 'The ideal of inner solitude in the twelfth century', in *Horizons marins: itinéraires spirituels (Ve-XVIIIe siècles)*, vol. 1 ('Mentalités et Sociétés'), ed. Dubois, Hocquet and Vauchez (Paris: Sorbonne, 1987) pp. 27–34.

263

As far as you are able, you have caused everyone to be lost. You set yourself between God and them, so that, by directing their gaze at you and forsaking God, they might admire, contemplate, and praise you alone. For you, and for them, this is utterly useless, not to say damning.

264

If you did not lack interior sights to see, you would never go out to look at exterior ones, or have leisure for them.

265

Your reading-glass has been broken, and you are upset. Blame yourself for this, and your own error, in attaching yourself to breakable things. A person has become so accustomed to putting the blame for all that is evil on something else that, if he hurts his foot against a stone or is burned by a fire, he has the audacity to blame and curse these things, which God created—things which, if they had not caused these events to happen, would justifiably be blamed for being impotent and lifeless—rather than deploring the unhappy plight of his own weakness.

Ps 91(90):12. Fully-fledged spectacles were not invented until c. 1290 in Venice: see A. Murray, *Reason and Society in the Middle Ages* (Oxford, 1978) p. 302.

266

Just as the young girl in the fable perished by staring at the sun, so will you by contemplating physical forms which are bound to perish, and human opinions too.

267

People try to create true pleasure or happiness for themselves in such a way as if either there were no such thing, or it were possible to create it—whereas it alone really exists but cannot by any means be created. To create happiness and God for yourself is the same thing as to believe that happiness and God do not exist at all.

268

If holding fast to God is the only wholly good thing for you, so being separated from him is the only wholly bad thing for you, and nothing else. This would be your Gehenna, this would be hell for you.

Ps 73(72):28

269

Ignorance is what causes the peace which is transient. If you understood perfectly the nature of transient things, you would never acquire them for your enjoyment or support.

270

To know, to praise, to esteem, to love, to enjoy something as if it were good, to admire, to respect—all these either benefit or harm the one who does them. For everyone's good depends on what he loves, esteems, and so on. But to be known, praised, esteemed, and so on, is a good thing not for the person being known or loved, but for the person who is doing these things. What good is done to the sun by the fact that people admire it? Or to the taste of honey, just because people love it so much?

271

The love with which we have been loved since before we existed, or for that matter when we were working iniquity, is the source of all our good.

272

Notice how you will willingly turn toward a grape or a mulberry without needing to be threatened by punishment; and you enjoy them wholeheartedly. But you won't turn toward him who made all these things, and you yourself, either after threats of eternal torments or after the promise of eternal happiness, which is he himself.

273

There is a sight which in this life is seen by no one's eyes apart, of course, from God's—and by yours insofar as you are capable of it: that is, how far your mind may be exalted above, or subject to, physical bodies or their forms, or human opinions and preferences.

274

The more each person holds fast to the highest good, the happier he is. Consequently the more he is separated from it, the more miserable he is. If the good that is lost is inexpressibly great, then so is the harm incurred. And if a greater good cannot be found, then neither can a greater harm be incurred.

275

Your habit and tonsure are an abiding deceit, for they stand for what you lack.

276

Nothing is to be yielded to covetousness, and nothing refused to love.

277

God has commanded human beings to love what they can never love too much. Contrariwise, human beings love above all else what they can never love too little.

278

When you ask God not to take away from you something you are greedily attached to, it is as if a woman, caught by her husband in the very act of adultery, were to ask him not to interrupt its delights when she ought to be seeking forgiveness for her offence.

279

It is not enough for you to be unfaithful to God: you even try to induce him to increase, preserve and provide those things whose enjoyment corrupts you—in other words, physical forms, tastes and colours—like a woman with the flesh of her adulterous lover.

280

What do you think of a person who devotes all his attention and time to shoring up a house which is beyond supporting, with materials none of which can possibly shore up anything— or, if they can, will themselves need just as many other supports as the house they are meant to be supporting, and those supports as many more, and so on *ad infinitum*? Wouldn't such a person be a poor fool?

Now life is that house, and you are the one who shores it up: the supports are transient things, which never stay as they are, and can never either support something else, or be supported themselves.

281

'It is you, Lord, who make me dwell only—in other words, completely—in hope.' Thus you have torn me away from all enjoyment and delight in things of the present.

Ps 4:10. In the Vulgate, the 'only' refers to the hope, whereas in the Hebrew original and in English translations it refers to the Lord: 'it is thou, Lord, only, that makest me dwell in safety'.

282

Notice how, when you recently tripped up in front of the brethren by singing one antiphon instead of another, your mind tried to think of a way of putting the blame on something else—on the book, or on some other thing. Your heart was reluctant to see itself as it really is, and so it pretended to itself that it was different, inclining itself to evil words to excuse its sin. The Lord will show you up, and set before you what you have done; and you will not be able to hide from yourself any longer, or to escape from yourself.

Ps 141(140):4, Ps 50(49):21

283

Human beings have not been commanded to create their own happiness, or their own god, but rather to obtain one that is not created but eternal. Only that can confer happiness on the human spirit—that is, only that form of being which causes the spirit to be and to live, to savour, to be at peace, to be secure, will certainly not lose any of these things. The person who does lack any of them is not happy.

284

Being devoid of God and far from him predisposes a person for evil cravings: the cravings predispose him for fear and sorrow, which is why we ought to fear and grieve over them all the more. So they are 'a wind that passes and comes not again'.

Ps 78(77):39

285

Nothing is more noble among creatures than spirits endowed with reason, especially those that are godly: nothing more vile than the corruptions of the flesh.

286

When you want people's admiration, and you are blinded by precisely that act of pride, consider how wretched you have become. Consider, then, the justice of God. For you have set yourself up as God to be admired by the noblest part of creation, and yet he has subordinated you to the lowest. You longed and did all you could, to make yourself known, seen, praised, admired and respected, loved and feared by everyone. Yet all these things should be owed by the noblest among creatures—in other words, uniquely by rational minds—only to God. So what has happened is just—namely that you,

who were setting yourself up as God to the noblest parts
of creation, accepted as a god what was most base in it; and
that you, who wanted (by perversely usurping God's place) to
extort from the noblest parts of creation what was due to God
alone, have offered what should have been given only to God
to the basest things of all—in other words, to corruptions of
the flesh and to corpses. On these things you bestow with
all your heart everything which should be given to God and
which you have set out above—love, and so on.

When, therefore, you usurp what belongs to God—being
praised, and so on—you have lost what belongs to man—
giving praise to God, for which you were created, and so
on. And because there is nowhere above the highest place or
below the lowest, as long as you strive to be above the highest
you have in fact been thrust down below the lowest. For it
is inevitable that if a person enjoys something, he will by his
love for it be subordinated to it. Now you enjoy the lowest
things. As a result you are thrust down below the lowest place,
where there is really no place at all. 'He is cast forth,' says the
Lord, 'like a branch.'

Jn 15:6

287

When you desire something good which depends on something else that is good, you do not escape misery but ac-
cumulate and increase uneasiness and need. Therefore you
must desire something good which does not depend on some
other good. All good things are such by virtue of the nature
of goodness. Therefore, everything needs goodness if it is to
be good. Yet goodness doesn't need anything else at all; for it
is good of itself. Love goodness, then, and you will be happy.

288

You were not created so as to be seen, or known, or loved, or
admired, or praised, but so as to see, know, love, admire and

praise the Lord. That alone, then, and nothing else, is good for you.

289

Power in this world is a useful thing, not to us, or for ourselves, but for our neighbors, either to protect them in temporal affairs, or to restrain them from evil by the fear of punishment. The same is true of eloquence.

290

A person who delights in some physical form ascribes the good things which seem to him to come from it, not to himself, but to it, and because of that he praises and loves it in his thoughts. So too he regards that form, and not himself, as good, and believes himself to be happy because of it. He no longer dwells in himself, but strives for it and draws towards it with a mental effort and willing assent in direct proportion to the enjoyment that makes him admire and delight in it. As a result, if someone harms or takes away that form, he regards the injury as something done to him and not to it. And because it was paradise and bliss for him to hold fast to this form, so it is hell and misery for him to be separated from it. This is how you are to live with respect to God.

291

When a person enjoys something to the full, he forgets himself and, so to speak, abandons and despises himself in order to strive for it: he pays attention not to what is happening in himself, but to what is happening in it; and he cares, not about what kind of a person he is, but about what kind of a thing it is.

The angels, therefore, despise themselves more than we do: directing themselves entirely towards God, they wholeheartedly abandon themselves and all other creatures with

them, and consider themselves so unworthy that they don't
even condescend to pay any attention to themselves there-
after. Indeed they despise themselves single-mindedly, forget
themselves, and hasten with all their hearts to him, paying
attention not to whom or what they are, but to whom he is.
And the more completely they despise and turn away from
themselves, the more they forget themselves, the more like
him they become, and thus the better they are.

292

'I will lie down in peace and take my rest'—in him who causes
the heavenly choir to sleep so that they stir no more, and
the heart to be neither troubled nor afraid. That is the true
sabbath.

Ps 4:9, Job 38:37, Jn 14:27

293

Either the doctor does not love the person who is sick, or he
heals him painlessly if he can, knowing that this is best for
him.

294

To whom could it be said in all truth: 'What do you have that
you did not receive' whereby he should glory in himself, and
not in the Lord? As Saint Gregory says, the more he becomes
aware of his obligation to render account, the more humble
he should be in respect of what he has been given. The more
he has received, the more he will owe.

1 Cor 4:7. The reference is to Gregory the Great, *Homilia in Evangelium*
9.1; PL 76:1106; CS 123:127.

295–6

(295) As long as someone loves the body and physical things,
the love which is life, light, freedom and a kind of boundless-
ness dies, is darkened, bound fast, and constricted. And just

as gold does not liquefy unless it is mixed with quicksilver, so too our mind remains inviolable and invulnerable unless it is mixed with love for corruptible and harmful things which cannot but change. But once it is mixed with them, it becomes as corruptible as they are, if not more so.

A small wound in the body, such as a flea-bite, causes great fear of suffering in the soul. Both your soul and your body are wounded by a flea-bite, the one by suffering, the other by being bitten. But you think that, when the bite on your body is healed, your soul is healed too, whereas the same weakness that made it yield to the wounded body still remains. Indeed, physical weakness cannot be healed in this life, and invariably tends to get worse; but spiritual health, if it does not begin here, will not be found at all in the life to come. (296) The only remedy for all pains and torments of this kind lies in making light of what has been hurt, and the conversion of the mind towards God.

297

Not much is gained if you take away from a person something that he holds onto wrongly; but it is if, by your encouraging words and your example, you get him to let it go of his own accord. For to be rid of evil is not praiseworthy; but to have got rid of it is.

298

Of his own free will a person entangles himself in the love of bodies and vanity; but whether he likes it or not he is tormented by fear and pain at their loss, whether it is caused by someone taking away the bodies he loved, or by someone disparaging them. The love of things that will perish is a kind of wellspring of worthless fears and pains, and of every form of stress. The Lord delivers the poor from the powerful by freeing him from the chains of worldly love. For the one who

loves nothing that will perish has nothing with which the powerful may harm him; and the one who loves only imperishable
things as they should be loved is entirely invulnerable.

Ps 72(71):12

299

If somebody were to cut off all the hairs on your head, he
would not hurt you unless he touched their roots. So too,
no one hurts you unless he touches the things that have
become rooted in you by means of your cravings: the more
numerous these things are, and the more they are loved, the
more numerous and violent will be the agonies to which they
give birth.

300

There is no security in pride, nothing exalted above God.
When, therefore, God pursues you in some way, you should
seek no succour in preference to him. How often you do what
the giants did, building a tower so as to sin with impunity!

For people only complain about one thing: that they cannot
achieve what they want, not that they don't want what is
good for them, or that they want what harms them. They
are distressed only because they lack the power to achieve
what they want; but whether it is good for them they do not
even consider. It is as though no error or harm could be in
the will, whereas on the contrary all the evils of humanity are
in the will alone.

Gen 11:4 and 6:4

301

Notice how you love your body incomparably more than it
is worth. Your distress is out of all proportion to the harm it
suffers. The smallest injury to it, such as a flea-bite, causes
you great stress.

But the person for whom God is the entire and sole good mourns the loss of him alone, and nothing else. Not so the rich man in hell: he bore his loss of God lightly, for he didn't ask for God to be restored to him. It was the refreshing water to which he was accustomed that he found hard to be without.

Lk 16:22–24

302

'The ear of the Lord hearkens to the disposition of your heart'; but you are ignorant of it, as was Saint Peter when he said: 'I am ready to go with you to prison and to death.' So do not value highly either your own or someone else's estimate of you, but God's alone.

Ps 10:19(9:37), Lk 22:33. Guigo may also have had in mind Ps 94(93):11.

303

Consider how ignorant you are about yourself. There is no region so remote and unknown to you, and about which you would more readily believe someone who told you lies.

R.W. Southern, *The Making of the Middle Ages* (London, 1953) 220–1, discusses this meditation in the context of the medieval monastic emphasis on self-knowledge.

304

The more unknown something is, the easier we judge it to be, and the more important the person telling you about it, the more easily we believe it.

305

Notice that, being united to this body of yours, you have been rather miserable. You have been exposed to all its weaknesses, even a flea or a mouse bite. But this was not enough for you: you have united yourself to other bodies, so to speak—people's opinions, admiration, love, honor, fear and other similar things; and the things that harm them cause you to suffer just as the things that harm the body do. You have thus provided yourself with the wood by which you will be burned. Just as your honor is undoubtedly wounded when you are disparaged, so it is when any of these other things are. It is in this way that you should also reflect on physical forms.

306

There are certain tastes, like that of honey; and there are certain temperaments and passions, like those of the flesh. When these things are taken away or damaged, notice how you feel about it.

307

Consider how poverty and squalor create solitude in the middle of cities, and wealth fills the deserts with crowds.

The word *eremus*, here translated 'desert', is used by Guigo in the *Consuetudines* to mean the monastic enclosure of the Chartreuse.

308

The greatest value of physical things consists in their use as signs. Many signs necessary for our salvation come from them, such as voices from the air, crosses from wood, baptism from water. Moreover, souls only know each others' feelings by means of physical signs.

309

Prepare yourself to submit to the law which you yourself enforce upon others. You are obliged to be subject to the laws you enacted, whether they are good or bad. The measure you give will be the same measure you get back. Thus you are to bestow upon others laws that are good and full of compassion, in case they are bad—which God forbid—and things go badly for you too, since you are subject to them. There will be judgment without mercy to one who shows no mercy.

Mt 7:2, James 2:13

310

The Lord has shown how contemptible are secular power and a long life in the flesh by giving Pontius Pilate the power to kill his son, and Nero the empire of the world, and also by giving to crows and deer many years of life. He rarely gives these things to the saints. When the Lord gives to any saint power over other people, he is having mercy on them, not on the saint. It is not the saint who needs subjects, but the subjects who need a good ruler.

Jn 19:10–11. Crows and deer were famed in the classical era for their longevity. (Hocquard, 'Les méditations. . . .' vol. 2, *Analecta Cartusiana* 112:2 [1987] 57–8).

311

To constrain and destroy an evil will has the same merit as to perfect and fulfil a good one. The latter is the work of angels, the former of holy people, in whom 'the spirit lusts against the flesh', and so on. Christ, who is truth, teaches each of these to both. There is the same merit in repentance as in innocence, though to a lesser degree.

Gal 5:17

312

To weep when you should weep, and to rejoice when you should rejoice: to hate evil, and to love good: to condemn the deed, and to love the doer: to withdraw from the adulterer, and delight in the Spouse: to persevere in what is good, and to return to it. Some of these actions are the work of human beings, some of angels; but one and the same spirit of Christ works them all.

Rom 12:15, Rom 12:9, 1 Cor 12:11

313

Try having a conversation with the things you delight in—if you can. And if you can't, be ashamed of yourself, you idolater!

314

You lack interior vision—vision of God—not because it is absent but because your interior sight is dim* and does not perceive it. The result is that you willingly leave your interior self behind in order to wander abroad. Furthermore, you cannot dwell within yourself because this feels to you like dwelling in darkness, and so you spend your time admiring either exterior physical forms or other people's opinions. You mustn't blame these physical forms for detaining or frightening you, or stirring you in some way: blame your own blindness, and the fact that you are devoid of the highest good.

*This phrase (in Latin *interius lippus*) is used on several occasions by Gregory the Great (e.g. *Homiliae in Ezechielem* 2.11, PL 76:954), and originates in the biblical description of Jacob's first wife Leah as being 'weak-eyed' (*lippis oculis*), Gen 29:17. See also the letter of Saint Bruno to Raoul le Verd, §6 (SCh 88:70).

315

Either extinguish cravings altogether, or prepare to be disturbed—in other words, to be afraid and to suffer when you oughtn't to do so.

316

Consider this: if all people give up everything else that interests them, and direct their entire attention towards one particular color or taste, how miserable, foul and stupid they will be. They are like that even now, when they are engrossed in so many diverse aspects of things. Neither a still greater multitude of created things, nor even the sum of them, constitutes our God or our salvation, any more than any one of them does.

317

All people endeavor to accomplish what they want. But who has assured them that what they want is either good or profitable? What could give them proof of this?

318

Those who of necessity will die one day, and who are sinners, try in vain to achieve two things: to live, and to keep themselves hidden. Both are impossible: all must necessarily die, and there is nothing covered that will not be revealed, and nothing hidden that will not be known.

Mt 10:26

319

The only person who genuinely worships God is one who really directs his attention to him, with feelings of genuine fear and love, honor and reverence, and wonder. This alone is true and perfect worship. Anyone who offers these sentiments to anything other than God is really an idolater.

Hence the apostle says 'Their god is their belly', and elsewhere 'For they that are like this serve not God, but their own belly', and again 'Greed is the service of idols'.

But doesn't the person who wants these feelings to be directed towards him frankly occupy the place of the devil, who tries by every means to extort these feelings from people? Thus almost all the complaints of people consist in this: that their gods—in other words, the created things to which they were offering this true and holy worship—either perish, or are taken away from them; or even that this kind of worship is not being offered to them.

Notice, then, the extent to which idolatry still holds sway in you and throughout the world.

Phil 3:19, Rom 16:18, Eph 5:5

320

A proud person accepts neither a superior nor an equal. There is in fact only one who has no equal or superior, and that is God—there cannot be two beings like that. So the proud person wishes to be God. But there cannot be two gods. So he wishes that God did not exist. With good reason, then, 'God resists the proud'.

James 4:6 and 1 Pet 5:5

321

When you see or hear evil things about other people, examine your own heart to determine how much genuine love you have for others.

322

Consider the extent to which you despise yourself. For there is almost nothing to which your mind and will do not more easily pay attention, and in which they do not more readily take their rest. 'Your soul cleaves to the dust, and your belly to the ground.'

Ps 119(118):25, Ps 44(43):25

323

A person who genuinely loves to be truthful, rather than appearing to be, and who is genuinely afraid of being a liar, rather than seeming to be one, refutes himself the moment he realizes he has lied, and no reproaches or fines can cause him to change his mind. He prefers to die in the truth rather than to live as a liar, if indeed a liar lives at all, since it is written 'A lying mouth deals death to the soul'. Consequently neither can the liar live, nor the truthful person die, as long as they remain thus. If the lying mouth deals death to the soul, the mouth that speaks the truth gives life to it. The truthful person lives, then, by what is true, and he lives by what it is that makes him truthful. So he lives by the truth, which is God; and he lives for ever, nourished by eternal food, which is truth itself.

Wis 1:11

324

You should not desire as a good something that itself needs another good. Its own need will increase yours, not remove it. It will therefore make you all the more miserable.

325

No object should want to be loved as a good apart from something which, by virtue of being loved, brings happiness to the person who loves it. But nothing does this, except something that doesn't need anyone to love it, in other words that gains no advantage either in being loved by someone, or in loving something itself.

Therefore an object which wants someone to focus on it his designs, his affection and his hope, when it cannot do him any good, is extremely cruel. This is what demons do: they want people to be employed in their service instead of in God's.

So you should cry out to those who love you: 'Stop admiring, revering or in any way honoring me at once, you unhappy people; for I, unhappy as I am, cannot be of any help either to myself or to you: on the contrary, it is I who need your help.'

326

Anyone who wants to enjoy you for your own sake deserves the same thanks from you as the flies and fleas that suck your blood.

Cf. Augustine, *De doctrina christiana* 1.3.4; CCSL 32:8, and Introduction, section 5

327

Notice how, in this sea, so to speak, of countless physical forms and human spirits which are always in a state of flux, you are never allowed to be still.

Job 14:2

328

To kill a human being is one thing, to kill an ungodly one is another. To kill a human being is to separate his soul from his body. But an ungodly person is not killed by any means unless his mind is transformed, his ungodliness condemned, and he becomes godly. Thus an ungodly person does not die when his body does. Similarly a just person does not die unless he becomes unjust—unless, that is, he abandons justice.

329

God should be loved in proportion to his nature and greatness. But he is eternal and infinite. Thus the love of someone who loves him in the manner and to the extent that he should is eternal and infinite. So the one who loves God is eternal and infinite himself. But no one can quite love God in the way, and to the extent, that he should, apart from someone who knows perfectly who and how great God is. But no one knows this except God himself. Consequently true eternity and true infinity do not exist except in him. Nevertheless, to the extent to which someone does this, he becomes like that himself—in other words, he becomes infinite and eternal.

330

The word 'judgment' is used to mean both 'condemnation' and 'discernment.' 'Do not judge' means not 'do not discern' but 'do not condemn.' Whether a person does good or evil, you are always to seek only his salvation. For it is wrong for you who need forgiveness yourself to condemn others who need it.

Lk 6:37

331

Not only should you accept no salary for doing your duty: you should not even be deterred by any adversities from doing it. You should eagerly seek justice for its own sake, as its own reward, and avoid wickedness for its own sake, even if no other punishment were to follow from it: it is, so to speak, its own punishment.

332

Just as no reward should make you yield to sin, so no loss should cause you to abandon justice.

333

Supposing those things that are imprinted in your mind, and to which you succumb out of admiration and love—honors that are due to God alone—were sculptures or paintings in some corner of a house, and you were to venerate them out of admiration or love, or by bowing your head to them: if people came to hear of it, what would they make of you?

334

Criticism precedes amendment. We are only allowed to change something that causes displeasure. Thus, because you are always in need of change, you always need to be displeasing to yourself.

335

Notice how these physical deformities affect your mind like a magnet and captivate it, as is written about Judith: 'The sandals of her feet took his mind prisoner'—the mind, that is, of Holofernes. Not his body first, but his mind; and, through the mind, his body too.

Jdth 16:11

336

From now on, you must wean yourself away from those physical forms: shame on you for not being able to be without them! And since, whether you like it or not, you will lose them some day, do now, willingly and with great reward or grace, what some day you will be obliged to do, and with great suffering too. Are you not going to give up this life and everything to do with it, even if no one takes it away from you? Look, everything is yours! Yet isn't it true that one day you will lose it all? Therefore, do now what you will do then, when you lose everything: that is, learn to be without these things; learn to live and rejoice in the Lord.

Cf. Jerome, Ep 22.41; ed. Labourt, 1:160; 'Begin to be now what you will be then'.

337

It is one thing to do or suffer what you want, another what is good for you. This is the verdict of the psalmist on the wicked: 'I gave them up to their own hearts' lusts'—in other

words, to what they wanted—'and they will follow their own
imaginations.' So too the insane person who chews his own
arms, or kills his parents or friends, undoubtedly does what
he wants, but not what is good for him. And the Lord said to
Peter: 'You will be led,' not where it is not good for him to
be, but 'where you do not wish to go'. Turn away, then, from
your own will. If you grant your spirit all it wants, as Scripture
says, 'it will make you a laughing-stock to your enemies'.

Ps 81(80):13, Jn 21:18, Si 18:30–1

338

Happy is everyone who does at least want what is good for
him. Can anyone, then, want what is not good for him, or
what is bad for him? If only once in your entire life you
would want what is good for you, as you ought to do! What a
wretched fate, not to be able not to want what is bad for you!

339–40

(339) When two things are equal, there are two ways in which
one can become greater than the other: by its own growth,
or by its neighbor's loss. By this latter way all princes and
secular authorities enjoy being greater than others, or strive
to become so—that is, by their degradation and loss, not by
raising or increasing themselves either physically or mentally.
Yet by that method neither their bodies nor their minds are
improved, even though they appear to themselves to have
progressed and increased because the others have declined
and decreased. For if everything were to be diminished so
much that it was reduced to nothing, how would that make
either your soul or your body grow?

(340) You should strive to be better than you are now, or in
other words to be better than yourself. Everything that genuinely makes progress becomes better than itself: this alone is
to its advantage. When reflecting on the genuine progress of
anything, we do not consider whether it is better than other

things, but whether it is better than itself, than it normally is. It could become greater than others by their decline rather than by its progress; but it can only become better than itself by means of its own advancement.

341

You should not rejoice if you happen to be better than the rest: instead you should lament the fact that they are not as good, and regard this as a deficiency on your part.

342

How is it that people do not glory or take pride in might or beauty when they do glory in weakness and wretchedness? They glory in these things if they ride a horse, or if their wretchedness is concealed by the elegance of their clothes, when they would really seem able to glory if they were to carry the horse by their own strength, or at any rate were not dependent on it—and if they adorned their clothes with their own splendour, or did not even need to have them adorned. These things and others like them testify to people's poverty and wretchedness.

Jer 9:23. Compare the story of Guigo with Saint Bernard's horse (*S. Bernardi Vita Prima* 3.4; PL 185:305).

343

'Friendship with this world,' as Saint James said, 'is enmity with God. Whoever, therefore, will be a friend of the world will be the enemy of God.' Anyone who loves just one fly in this world necessarily loves the entire world, because the whole world is necessary for the existence of the one thing that he loves. Furthermore, for as long as love of this world exists, there will be enmity between God and humanity. So when you want to be loved by people, you want them to become enemies of God.

However, when you preach you tell people to despise whatever is created so that they may be reconciled to God. Are you therefore going to make an exception only of yourself, and say to people: 'For God's sake despise everything, except me', so that nothing except you hinders their reconciliation with God, and enmity persists between God and humanity solely because of you? Surely no one can be saved while they are obliged, by loving you, to love the whole world, which is necessary for your existence?

Now it is one thing to love people in the world or because of the world, another to love them in God or on his account. The former is cupidity, the latter compassion.

James 4:4

344

How readily a person would show off his own beauty, if he had any, as he shows off that of other things, like his clothes, or furs, or anything else!

Si 11:4. Cf. Ezek 16:15ff.

345

Everything which genuinely makes progress is changed for the better, either in part, or entirely; and we chart the course of its progress, either as a whole, or in one particular area. When we want to improve it, we work to change it, either wholly or partially. It is the same with something that deteriorates.

What, then, is this madness which plagues our human race? Who among human beings devotes himself to what is good for him? Which soul tries to change itself for the better? What mad intoxication! For when we indulge ourselves in this world through the openings of this carnal vessel—in other words, through the body's senses—we attach ourselves to its various parts; and so, with our mind's attention distracted from ourselves, we marvel at those things that are changed for

the better or worse, by us or by others, counting their progress
as our own. Thus, deservedly, and with a kind of inexpressible
folly, we reckon their progress to be ours, because, as we get
more familiar with them, we come to know them, and yet
do not know ourselves. For what soul nowadays is ignorant
of what is white or black, or of some such thing? Yet what
soul knows itself? If you were to ask all human souls what
those things are, they will answer effortlessly and uniformly,
as they would of things they know. If, however, you were
to ask them what they themselves are, in other words what
the soul is, they would immediately be confused: some would
say they don't know what it is, others that it consists of fire,
others of air, others of a fluid, others of something else, while
unquestionably if it is one of those things it cannot possibly
be any of the others. So this diversity of opinions only goes
to show that they have no idea what the soul is.

They should be ashamed, then, since they know so much
about other things but do not know themselves. They should
be ashamed because they are certain about some things, but
uncertain about themselves. They marvel at things that are
meaner than they are, and rely on things that are inferior.
And yet, from all these things, they cannot even create one
hair on the body which each carries about.

346

You shouldn't try to get your lords—in other words, your
Lord's children—whom you have been appointed to serve by
the Lord your God, their father, to do what you want, but
what is to their advantage. You should be seeking what is good
for them rather than their doing what you want, since they
have been entrusted to you not so that you can rule over them
but so that you can do them good.*

In the same way a sick person is entrusted to a doctor, not to
be ordered around, but to be healed. The doctor is not against
the sick person, but on his side, which means being against his
illness; and he regards the sick person's health as complete and

sufficient compensation for everything the person has caused him to endure. He doesn't blame the person for anything: he blames the illness, and so gets his full revenge by disposing of the illness.

*The contrast between 'ruling' and 'doing good' (Latin *praesum* and *prosum* respectively) had become a familiar one in monastic literature from the time it was employed by Saint Benedict (RB 64:8) with reference to the abbot of a monastery. See also, among many other patristic references, Gregory the Great, *Moralia in Iob* 21.15; PL 76:203. Part of this Meditation has been incorporated in the *Statutes of the Carthusian Order* (23:22).

347

'Let the just man correct me out of pity', as someone who suffers with me because I have fallen: not out of justice, as someone giving me what I deserve. For he himself would not want to be given what he deserved. If he acts otherwise, with a different motive, he is not just: he will not be doing to someone else what that person needs, or what he wants someone to do to him.

Ps 141(140):5

348

The woman who neither fornicates, nor deserts her own husband, simply because she has not discovered an adulterous relationship that will last, is not avoiding adultery but looking for a lasting one. But you, on top of all your wickedness, have mentally stretched open your legs to every passer-by, to enjoy momentary acts of adultery for lack of more enduring or eternal ones.

Ezek 16:15 and 16:25. Both verses in the old (*Vetus Latina*) text have *crura* instead of *pedes tuos* after *divaricasti*. Guigo may not have known this old translation; but he will have known Jerome, Ep 96.12, where it is quoted (ed. Labourt, 6:20).

349

Four people were entrusted to two doctors: the first received one healthy person and one sick person, and the second the other healthy person with the other sick one. Payment was promised for looking after them, with a view either to restoring or to preserving their health.

So one doctor did for those entrusted to him everything that should have been done to look after them or restore them to health; but nonetheless they died. The other doctor did none of the things that ought to have been done, and yet the healthy person remained healthy and the sick one recovered. Which of them deserved payment—the one whose patients both died, or the one whose patients are alive and well?

Without any doubt the one who did what he should from motives of integrity is no less worthy of praise and reward than he would have been if his patients were alive and well. But the one who was unwilling to do what he should is no less deserving of punishment than he would have been if his patients had died.

350

A sick person is not entrusted to a doctor for the doctor to do what he likes to him, but to do what is good for him: nor is he entrusted so that the doctor can dominate him, but so that he can heal him.

351–2

(351) There were two doctors: one gave a sick person whom he secretly hated a potion which he thought would be fatal to him; and the person was healed. The other, from motives of sincere love, gave his dearest friend a drink which he thought would do him good; and he died.

Whether someone's will is perfectly good or bad, it will be judged by the result; and as there is peace on earth to people of good will, so there is labor and sorrow for those of evil intent. Thus it often happens that the person who has killed someone is regarded as a healer, and the person who has healed someone as a murderer.

(352) Two things, then, go to make an excellent doctor: good intentions, and perfect knowledge. It is not in his power to heal everyone entrusted to him. No one, after all, can know which patients are incurably ill, and which have a chance of recovery. The doctor must care for everyone, and apply all his skill to each person with total devotion. By doing this we shall deserve from the Father of all no less grace and reward for those who have died than for those who are healed.

Lk 2:14, Ps 90(89):10

353

'In your splendor and your beauty make haste, ride on in triumph, and reign.' In other words, if you make haste towards someone else's—that is, towards outward—beauty, you will not ride on in triumph and reign: instead you will serve the creature rather than the Creator, who is himself the splendor and beauty of the rational and godly mind.

Ps 45(44):5

354

The Pharisee should not have said: 'God, I thank you that I am not like other people, or even like this publican', but 'I am not my usual self.' For the latter are the words of someone making progress, and acknowledging God's grace, whereas the former are the words of a boaster who makes rash judgments about the secrets of another person's heart.

Lk 18:11

355

The vice for which this or that person despised you is the same one for which you, swollen-headed as you are, grieved at being despised—in other words, pride. And the vice which caused someone to take away what was yours is the same as what caused you to lament its loss—in other words, love of things that will perish.

356

Happy the person whose mind is moved or affected only by knowledge and love of the truth, and whose body only by his mind. In this way his body too is moved only by the truth, because if no one's mind were moved except by the truth, and no one moved in body except by the mind, no one would be moved in body except by the truth—in other words, by God.

357

It would be a merciful punishment if a husband, catching his wife in the act of adultery, only took from her the opportunities she had for fornication. But how impudent and shameless she would be if she were to regard that as an injustice! Now you have hardly any cause for grief except the same one, in other words, the removal of your opportunities for fornication. Your grief convicts you of fornication, so that there is no need of further witnesses.

Mk 14:63

358

However shameless and impudent a woman is, she tends to hide from her husband's eyes these things: the tears she sheds for the misfortunes that befall her lover, and the ones she sheds for the injuries done to her by her lover in anger—as well as the injuries themselves, and her delights too.

Now consider whether you do at least as much with regard to God. If you do not grieve openly before him over the

misfortunes of your lover—in other words, of this world—
then you rejoice over its prosperity. So 'you had a whore's
forehead'.

Jer 3:3

359

You recognize what things should be given to God alone in
the fact that, if they are offered to any object at all, they
do it no good—such as knowledge, the love that leads to
fruition, admiration, fear, reverence, and so on. These things
prove, since they bring no advantage to the person to whom
they are offered, that they ought to be given to him alone
who needs none of them. If to be praised, or to be known,
or to be admired were advantageous, who would not hire
people as workers, paid daily, who would offer these things to
him constantly, so that he would benefit all the time? What
mother would not do this unceasingly to her own children?
Who would not compliment his own clothes, his property, his
animals and himself by singing their praises day and night, so
as to improve them?

All these things, then, are of no value to the one to whom
they are addressed; but the person who offers them becomes
either worse or better by virtue of offering them. If he loves
or admires or fears what he should, he becomes better; but
if he does this with regard to what he shouldn't, he certainly
becomes worse. So it is with all of these things.

How good, then, is the Lord, who demands nothing from
us for his own benefit and yet considers it a great service if
we always do what conduces to our good!

360

If an image of dung were made of gold, it would certainly
be better in substance than in image—its substance would
be gold, but its image dung. However, if the image of an
angel were cast in gold, it would be better in image than in

substance—its image would be that of a living, spiritual and rational substance, but its substance a senseless and lifeless body. So, when your mind is moved with love for physical, lifeless and perishable things, it is clearly better in substance than in image. In substance it is a life endowed with reason, made in the image of God; but its image is the same as what it is concerned with and enjoys. So when it indulges itself through the senses of the body, and strives for these things, it in fact departs from what is better—in other words, the living and rational substance which is its own self—and strives for what is worse. And the more passionately it does this, the worse it becomes.

However, when it gives full rein to what is above itself, and is moved by the truth—in other words, by God—it is much better and more precious in form than in substance. In substance it is a soul, but in form (if I can put it like this) it is God. 'For I have said, "You are gods, and children of the Most High".' When, therefore, the soul reaches out from itself towards him, it goes from what is worse to what is better than anything; and the more efficaciously it does this, the better it becomes.

Ps 82(81):6

361

Rejoicing when you shouldn't is the same kind of misery as grieving when you shouldn't; and yet the one causes the other. Foolish joy gives birth to foolish sadness. Because an adulterous woman takes a perverse pleasure in the embrace of her lover, she grieves perversely when he is snatched from her. Both states of mind are equally depraved, and equally unfortunate.

362

Just as no idolater could create a god equal to himself, since as a living human being 'he was fashioning a dead thing with wicked hands', so neither could he create something good—happiness, pleasure, or security—whether in the form of food, drink, clothes, or protective fortifications. These are dead things made by living people. People who are utterly wicked find nothing which could be their equal in this happiness which they reckon as theirs. They could not possibly enjoy these things, which they abuse by finding pleasure in them contrary to God's command, if they were not of greater worth than the things were.

This is precisely the height of human depravity: to abandon what is better than you are—in other words, God—and to aspire and hold fast to what is more wretched—in other words, transient things—by enjoying them.

Wis 15:17

363

Christ leads the angels to the embrace of their spouse: he snatches us from our adulterer, the world. He makes them strong and steadfast so that they can enjoy the spouse, which is he himself: he makes us the same so as to set us free from our adulterer, the world. He holds them fast in sight or reality: he holds us fast in faith and hope. He gives them perfect joy in true happiness: he gives us patience in tribulation. He gives them a happy life, but to us a most precious death. He lets them live for him, for God: he lets us die to the world. To them he grants joy in the good things that are theirs: to us, grief over the evils that are ours; to them, joyful hearts: to us, contrite ones; to them, justice: to us, repentance; to them, the perfection of goodness: to us, its beginning.

Cf. 2 Cor 5:7, Ps 116(115):15, Ps 51(50):19. The first sentence reads literally 'to the embrace of his [i.e. Christ's] spouse'. For an analysis of this meditation, see the Introduction, pp. 18–19; and also Hocquard, 'Les méditations . . .' vol. 2, *Analecta Cartusiana* 112:2 (1987) 63–4.

364

I swear confidently that the angels have received from God no greater or nobler gift, nothing more precious or profitable, and so nothing more desirable or beautiful, than love. Who understands or believes this? 'God is love', and so someone who possesses something greater or better than love possesses something greater and better than God.

1 Jn 4:16

365

Notice that when you paint, or do something similar, you take for your model another object that you have seen at some time, or can see now. But what did God look at to help him create all things? What other sun, or other world? Where did he see these things, so as to be able to make them? He created everything, then, by himself, by his own power, his own wisdom, his own kindness—in other words, by his mercy. No one helped him, no one instructed him, and no one gave him advice.

366

Try exposing to the sun's ray one ball made of clay, and another of wax. Although there is only one ray, it cannot have the same effect on both: it works differently on each, depending on their inner state—hardening the first, and liquefying the second. For it can neither liquefy the one that is made of earth, nor harden the one made of wax.

So too, the one outward appearance of a metal—let us say gold—when seen by several people, arouses different reactions in them depending on the state of their minds. One person is fired with a desire to carry it off, another to steal it, another to give it away to the poor. A foolish person declares that the one who possesses it is happy: a wise person grieves for the one who loves it. It can neither awaken evil intentions in a good mind, nor good intentions in an evil one; but the appearance of this and of other physical or material objects, or what causes them, affects human minds entirely in relation to the inner state of those minds. Consequently, the sole cause of our wickedness should be blamed on us, not on the things through which we sin. In effect, then, they do nothing for us other than to put us to the test: they reveal what we were like in secret, but they do not make us thus.

For the firmness and constancy of the love with which a wife holds fast to her husband is proved by the way she looks at other men: if she is genuinely chaste, she is not excited by anyone else's good looks. So too with you: if you were to hold fast to God with the firmest affection, you would not be seduced by the sight of any creature. All these things reveal the extent of your chastity towards God.

367

I would like to know if you regard as fools those who, at the sight of a ball, a sickle* or a little bird, or any such trifling thing, are moved to desire it passionately. Now observe how much you yourself are affected when you see or imagine such things.

*conjectural translation. The word *(h)arpa* derives from the Greek *harpê* (=a sickle). In later Latin it came to mean a harp; but 'sickle' seems to fit the context better here.

368

If you ask people why they are miserable—whether it is because they do not want what would be good for them, or because they do not have what they want—they will answer at once: it is because they cannot have what they want. However, this is just another way of saying: 'We are enlightened people: we know very well what is good for us, and we like it; but we are weak.' This is nonsense. For who is there, among all those living in the world, who loves something which can make him better? People only desire things which are of less value than they are. And how can something which is better, more precious and more noble be improved by what is worse, more wretched, and more ignoble?

369

Alas! How many people do what they like: how few want what would be good for them even if they achieved it! And yet who will ever be able to persuade the sons of Adam of this? When will they admit that they do not love what is good for them, since they are ready to swear that they don't desire anything evil for themselves, and that everything they suffer in all their efforts they are enduring for their own good?

It is as if you were to tell an idolater that he isn't worshipping God. He would leap up at once, swearing that he does worship God, recounting how much he devotes to worship, and even pointing his finger at the god he worships. Nevertheless, he does not worship God but what, deceived by error, he takes to be God.

So people undoubtedly do not love or desire what is good for them, but what they mistakenly believe to be good for them; and as a result they think that whatever they do or suffer for this thing, they are doing or suffering for their own good.

370–1

(370) The only person who desires and loves what is good for him is the person who loves God. For God alone is the entire and only good of human nature. Indeed it is written that 'he who abides in love'—in other words, he who loves God—'abides in God and God abides in him'. This, then, is true human fulfilment: no one can love it other than the one who possesses it; and it can never on any account be separated from the one who loves it.

(371) The very fact, then, that people say they certainly do love what is good for them—and who would not be prepared even to swear to this?—but do not possess it: this very fact, I

say, proves that they love something else, and not their own fulfilment. All someone has to do in order to possess what is good for him is to love it. Yet these people constantly try to create it, as though it did not exist, which is what the pagans try to do with God. For if God alone is the fulfilment of humanity, and only someone who does not love him at all can be without him, this fulfilment cannot be created because it is eternal: it can only be loved.

This alone, then, is the cause of all our misery: that either we don't recognize and love our own fulfilment, or we don't recognize and love it as much as, or in the way that, we should recognize and love it.

1 Jn 4:16

372

Consider the thornbush: after it springs up here, it immediately puts roots down wherever its branches reach. In the same way your soul puts down roots of love in many clods of earth and clings to them with the utmost tenacity—first to this body of yours, and then to others. It also clings to, and depends on, human opinions and preferences.

Guigo may have had in mind here Isaiah 32:13, which refers to thornbushes springing up on the soil of God's people.

373

Bear in mind the different ways of recognizing God by reflecting on created things: through established signs, like crosses, words, and so on; and through natural signs, like a sudden flush or pallor of the face, and so on. Some of these signs are of physical things, some of spiritual ones.

374

The will* to do things, unaccompanied by either wisdom or power, is both folly and torment at the same time. Folly

is wanting what you should not: torment is being unable
to do what you want. The will accompanied by power, but
without wisdom, is unfettered frenzy, hurtling first to its own
destruction and then destroying everything else.

*omitting 'and power' with mss. M,T,B and P

375

Fields, walls, houses, meadows, woods, vineyards and other
things of this world ought to want you, Guigo, to fulfil your
wishes, for that is to their advantage. This is because you
desire and work to improve them, either by adding what
they need and* will do them good, or by changing them
for the better. But you, Guigo, should not want things to
turn out as you wish. You neither desire nor work to improve
yourself—in other words, this soul and body of yours—either
by adding what is really beneficial, or by changing it for the
better: instead you devote all, or almost all, your efforts to
experiencing through your bodily senses external phenomena
and whatever pertains to them.

*Reading *et* with mss M,T,B and P; G has *aut*

376

Supposing two events took place, neither of which you witnessed: both are described to you, and you regard both as
equally possible. To which do you attach more credence? The
one which is described by people whom you believe to be
of greater authority, and to be more truthful—especially if
there are many of them. But what has more numerous, and
more authoritative, witnesses, than the fact of eternal life and
death? All the martyrdoms, fastings and labors, as well as the
zeal in words and deeds of all the elect since the beginning
of the world—in short, all the elect of the human race—bear
witness to these things. There is nothing, therefore, which
you should believe more, and more firmly. But think: do you
do this?

377

Notice how we are to seek transient things from God. Christ
the Lord said: 'Father, if you are willing, remove this cup from
me.' This is what you must say when it comes to obtaining
all the good things of this world, and avoiding the evil ones;
and with your whole heart add what follows: 'Nevertheless
not my will, but yours, be done'.

Cf. Lk 22:42 and Mk 14:36 (Guigo's Biblical references are rarely exact);
Mt 26:39.

378

Notice how suffering switches from body to soul, and from
soul to body. A wound in the body causes sadness in the soul;
and sadness shrivels and contracts the body, frequently making
it dissolve into tears.

379

The soul asks what the soul is, which is the same as whiteness
asking what whiteness is. The soul should be ashamed, then,
that it does not know itself, since it knows so many other
things; and nothing is more present to it than itself.

380

When we rejoice for the same reasons as animals do—from
wantonness, like dogs, or from greed, like pigs, and so on—
our souls become like theirs; and yet we are not horrified. For
myself, I would prefer to have the body of a dog than its soul.
However, if our bodies were changed so that they resembled
those of dogs to the same extent as our souls through wanton
behavior come to resemble dogs' souls, who would put up
with us, and who would not be horrified? It would be better,
and more bearable, for our bodies to be transformed into
wild beasts while our souls retained their dignity—that is, the

image of God—than for the body to remain human and the soul to become bestial. Certainly this latter transformation is as much more horrible and deplorable as the soul is superior to the body, which is why David said: 'Do not become like horse and mule, which have no understanding'. For we must not suppose that this is said about a physical likeness, which would be ridiculous!

Ps 32(31):9. Cf. Augustine, *Enarrationes in Psalmos* 29.2 (CCSL 38:176), 42.6 (CCSL 38:479), and 54.3 (CCSL 39:657).

381

It is easier to do something good than to do it well—in other words, to do it as it should be done, with the right intention. An act of love is frequently performed without love, as when you correct your neighbour out of insolence or dislike. In fact, when the same thing happens to us, we cannot believe it is done out of love because we don't like it. Similarly someone who is mentally unbalanced does not believe that he is being restrained, cauterized, or operated on out of love, because these actions terrify him.

382

People find it hard to believe that what upsets them may be done out of love.

383–6

(383) Take two idolaters: one rejoices because his idols are standing upright and thriving; the other laments because his have fallen over, and he is sad about it. Which, I ask you, is more wretched or wicked: the joy of the first, or the sorrow of the second? Aren't both to be abominated, and both utterly disastrous? Nevertheless, the second person would not have experienced perverse sadness if it had not been preceded by perverse joy. The joy, then, is more detestable, because it

is itself both perverse and evil—by corrupting the mind it disposes it for a sadness just as perverse as it is. This is why the original error is to be detested most, for if it had not come first, neither the perverse joy nor the perverse sadness would have followed.

(384) This, then, is why you should grieve as much for someone who rejoices at acquiring transient things as for someone who mourns their loss. Both are afflicted by the same fever: love of the world. (385) So God is no less merciful when he takes away these transient things as when he bestows them.

(386) If there were a very wise man who knew, by divine inspiration, the hidden secrets of humankind, as well as what was to be to the advantage of each person, then this man (if he existed) would exercise his compassion just as much by taking away those transient things as by bestowing them; and he would do that to ensure that foolish people did not become even worse by misusing them.

In the same way, if someone knew the future, it is possible that he could show more compassion and kindness by killing someone than by letting him live. If only Judas had died one day before conceiving his crime! However, this can never be allowed, because we do not know what each person will become in the future, and we ought to be optimistic about them all.

Yet even if this were not the case, even if we had to despair of their salvation altogether, they should still not be removed from our midst. In this world evil people do to good ones what fire does to gold in the furnace. The ungodly live, then, for the sake of the godly. And while it would once have been better for such a person, not only not* to have lived long, but not even to have been born—as is said of Judas in the Gospel—nevertheless he does not die, so that he can serve the Lord unwittingly by purifying the just through the fire of suffering. 'The Assyrian', said the Lord, 'is the rod of my anger', even though he didn't realize it.

So the rod must not be done away with altogether, as long as a child in need of chastisement** remains. The Lord said:

'By your patience you will possess your souls', and 'from good ground he has brought forth fruit with patience'. Yet what good will this be without suffering, since 'suffering produces patience', in order that we may be perfect?

It is not reprehensible, then—indeed it is good—that in this world power is in the hands of evil people, so that the just, while being subjected to them, may be oppressed, purified, tested, and crowned. Anyone who is angry about this would also be angry that grapes and olives are subjected to the wine or oil-press, and wheat to the thresher. Which, I might well ask, should be subjected to which: the press to the grapes and olives, or grapes and olives to the press?

*lit. "not only to have lived long"
**disciplina: see Introduction, page 52

Is 10:5, Lk 21:19, Lk 8:15, Rom 5:3. Cf. Augustine, *De vera religione* 27.50; BA 8:94: 'For the ungodly person lives for the sake of the godly, and the sinner for the just . . . .'

387*

You should not rejoice when something is acquired, either for you or for anyone else. 'You shall love your neighbour as yourself.'

*omitted in four of the five early mss

Mt 19:19

388

You should neither rejoice with someone when he acquires some object, nor commiserate with him when he loses it. For example: you should not share the joy of an adulteress when she gets what she wants, which is why you also should not commiserate with her when she laments her loss of the same thing.

389

Two people have been entrusted to you: one is ill, but curable; the other healthy, but susceptible to illness. Which should receive more care—the healthy person or the one who is sick? Surely you should be taking care and trouble as much to prevent the former from becoming ill as to enable the latter to recover, especially as all healthy people are much more likely to fall ill than the sick to get better? However, you should not lose hope over anyone's illness, nor become complacent about someone who is fit. For it is written: 'Do not praise a man during his lifetime, for you know not what tomorrow may bring'. Similarly it could and should be said: do not condemn someone while he is alive, for you know not what tomorrow may bring.

Prov 27:1

390

You can know, with God's help, what every human soul ought to be like. However, you cannot know perfectly what any soul is like, not even your own. Every rational soul ought to be totally devoted to God, since it is written: 'You shall love the Lord your God with all your heart', and so on. It should also be kind to its neighbor, for the text continues: 'and your neighbor as yourself'. And this is its entire and only perfection and salvation: no other affection should stir human hearts other than that twofold love, as it were. This must be the entire and only cause of all human actions and movements, whether spiritual or physical, down to the least wink of the eye or movement of the finger. But who is equal to this? Even so, it is for this that we must strive.

Now the works of devotion* to God are these: contemplation, prayer, meditation, reading, psalmody, celebration of the holy mysteries. The purpose of all these is to know and to love God.

The works of fraternal love are these: not imputing sin, intercession, dispensing the sacraments, word, example, and discipline**; in addition, the generous provision of bodily necessities, such as food, drink, clothing, shelter, medicine, burial, and whatever else is needed. Moreover, the 'word' is to be one of teaching, of encouragement (that is, of advice), of consolation, of correction, or of rebuke.

Devotio means more than interior piety: it summarizes all the practical outworkings of our love for God. See the remarks on this Meditation by J. Chatillon, article 'Devotio', in *Dictionnaire de Spiritualité* 3 (1955) cols. 710–1.
**disciplina*: see Introduction, page 52

Mt 22:37–39. For a detailed study of this Meditation, see Mursell (1988) 145–58.

391

There are two things that prove someone to be just, or point him out: the way he does things, and the way he suffers. It is not because he gave bread to the poor, or did something similar, or because he endured some insult with equanimity, that he is just: on the contrary, it is because he was just that he did these things. In other words, these actions don't make him just: as a just person, he does them. Even if he didn't physically do or endure these things, he would be no less just—and so it will be in the next world too. So he is just because he deeply desires, for himself and others, that life in which none of these things will have to be done or endured, for all human errors and weaknesses will have been taken away.

392

Consider what it is for someone to have received the power to do what he wants, when all he wants are things that are either worthless or pernicious. Isn't this the same thing as depriving a stupid boy of discipline* and letting him squander

his time uselessly; or depriving an insane person who wants
to kill himself of the chains which bind him?

disciplina: see Introduction, page 52

393

'You who fashion hardship into a commandment', as the pot-
ter fashions clay into a jar, means you who make a commandment for me out of that very hardship, so that I can
mentally escape from the things which cause me hardship.
I would not be suffering hardship if I had not withdrawn
from you, for 'you chastise people for sin'. But I, in my
perversity, long to escape, not from the wickedness for which
I am beaten, but from the rods themselves. Yet spiritually I
should oppose not the beatings, but what causes them—in
other words, wickedness.

Ps 94(93):20, Ps 39(38):12

394

Notice how much it matters to the sons of Adam to be able
to do what they want, and how little they care what it is that
they want, as if they could never be mistaken. Notice too
the number and extent of the hardships they undergo for a
doubtful hope, indeed for certain despair—in other words,
for things which may never come about, and which would be
bound to perish even if they did. These things come not to
abide, but of necessity to pass away.

395

'It is not you who speaks,' says the Lord, 'but the Spirit of your
Father who speaks in you'. Say this whole-heartedly about all
good works, to all good people. In other words, it isn't you
who offer bread to the poor, when you do this well—which
means in simplicity of heart—but the Spirit of your Father

who offers it through you. This and similar actions are done
well only through the love 'which is spread abroad in our
hearts through the Holy Spirit which is given to us'.
Mt 10:20, Rom 5:5

396

Notice how you are sad and upset, and grumble about this or
that person, because he spoke to you with words that were
insolent and full of malice. You are grieving, then, either
because of what he said or because of the attitude of mind
with which he said it. You are quite right, if you are grieving
for his benefit, for his action does him no good. But you are
wrong if you are grieving for yourself. He could have said
nothing which would benefit you more, nothing as holy and
profitable, or in so holy and profitable a way, as what he did
say, provided you make good use of it.

For whether someone says or does something good or bad
to you, in a good or a bad way, its value for you will depend
on the use to which you put it. However, for the person who
said or did it, its value will depend on his intention in saying
or doing it. Just as 'wickedness lies only to itself', and not
to you, provided that you disagree with it and refute it, so
too it does and says all these evil things to itself, to its own
detriment, provided that with godliness and compassion you
don't agree with it, but refute it.

You should grieve, then, for the person who did or said this
evil to you, not for yourself. The evil actions of someone else
even turn to good effect if you make good use of them—and
the better use you make of them, the more good they will
yield. So too, the worse use you make of what was done or
said to you, the more evil it will yield, irrespective of whether
it was good or bad in itself, 'for all things work together for
good for those who love God'—all things, even to the extent
of another person's evil. For those who hate God, everything
by contrast works together for evil—all things, even the good.

You should address all complaints, then, to yourself, for
making the wrong use of these things. Even if the things done

or said to you really are evil, they certainly cannot in any way
be so for you unless you use them badly. So too, though, good
things will not do you any good unless you put them to good
use.

Cf. Ps 27(26):12, Rom 8:28

397

When the Lord wants to destroy or strike down physical and
transient things, he proclaims and announces beforehand that
he is going to do it, so that we can detach ourselves from
them, and not perish or be struck down with them.

This may be a reflection on Gen 19:15–17.

398

A good doctor treats his patients with both bitter and sweet
things, like honey and wormwood, as well as with hard and
soft, and rough and smooth ones, but always with the same
intention, which is his desire to heal them. He does not
administer things because they are bitter or unpleasant, which
would be an act of cruelty, but because they are therapeutic,
which is an act of love.

The reference to the doctor administering wormwood and honey comes
from Lucretius, who is quoted by Jerome, Ep 133.3; ed.Labourt 8:53.

399

The human soul is justifiably tormented for as long as it can
be, in other words for as long as it loves something else more
than God. No one can lose God without wanting to do so.
Thus one can refuse God, but not lose him: 'no one is hurt
except by his own action.'*

*The title of a treatise by Saint John Chrysostom, PG 52:459–80, which
Guigo would have read in an ancient version: Wilmart, 'Les pensées . . .'
p. 149 n. 399; Laporte, SCh 308:260, n. 399(2).

400

Just as a child, from a small amount of clay, makes balls that
are as round and attractive as he could make from a large
amount, so a person who is just and wise creates something
that is no less just and pleasing to God from slender resources
as from extensive ones. Remember the widow's two mites, and
the cup of cold water.

Lk 21:2, Mt 10:42

401

Since you are one of God's creatures, like the others in the
sense of having a physical form, and yet incomparably more
noble and precious than all of them, why do you pay more
attention to them than they to you? Why do you burn with
desire for them more than they do for you? Why do you
thrust yourself on them more than they do on you? Why can
you not live without them, when they manage without you?
It is unquestionably you who can be of benefit to them, rather
than they to you—just as the idolater is of benefit to the idol,
not the idol to him.

402

Consider what happens when something is craved for the sake
of something else, such as wormwood for the sake of health—
or is hated because of something else, as honey usually is for
fear of illness. In the first case, we willingly accept the distress
in the present that is caused by its bitter taste, in the hope
of joy in the future arising from good health: in the second
case, we dread the pleasure in the present that is caused by
its sweetness, for fear of suffering in the future as a result
of being ill. When this happens, we do not crave or dread
the thing itself, but the thing on whose account we crave or
dread it. Take away the advantage of being healthy and who

wouldn't recoil from wormwood? Take away the fear of illness and who wouldn't crave the honeycomb?

So too, people very often hate wickedness, like theft or adultery, not on its own account, but because of the penalty that accompanies it, which is other people's scorn: take that away, and theft and adultery will soon become acceptable. That seems to be, at least partly, the reason why people do dread it—because other people's scorn is aroused by such things.

Ps 22(21):7. For wormwood and honey, see the note to Meditation 398.

403

Everyone senses instinctively what his own intention is towards the things he loves or respects, and what it is towards the things he despises or hates. This is why the wicked, whoever they may be, set their hearts on being loved and respected by people, so as to receive from them what people customarily offer to those they love and respect. So too they have a horror of being despised and hated by people, for fear of being deprived of these things, and of incurring instead whatever people normally inflict on those they despise and hate.

404

When someone is sorry for having stolen something, because thereby he has incurred people's scorn, he doesn't repent because he has committed theft, but grieves because of the scorn he has incurred. It is not the act of sinning, but the fact of being punished, that he hates and regards as evil.

For just people, however, there is no difference between committing a sin and being punished. They regard the sin itself as a most appalling punishment, so that no wickedness can be unpunished because wickedness itself is a great punishment, and nothing worse than that can be inflicted on anyone. For that reason the just think they should shun and flee from

wickedness before all other evils, even if no other evil were
to follow from it.

Ps 22(21):7

405

Someone who thinks that by loving worldly things he is loving
God is mistaken. Not only does that already mean he does
not love him: it means he also hates him. Friendship of this
world, then, is enmity with God; and whoever wishes to be
a friend of this present age thereby makes himself an enemy
of God.

James 4:4

406

'All the gods of the nations are demons'; but yours are not
even that. Demons are endowed with rational life, albeit aber-
rant, and will never cease to exist. But the objects which you—
and beasts—enjoy are dead and necessarily perishable. Not
even all of them together can match one live pig, let alone a
demon (which is an angel, though a perverse one).

Ps 96(95):5

407

A person who wants to make bricks prepares a yard where
he can put them temporarily, not of course for them to stay
there, but so that they can be moved somewhere else when
they have dried. Thus the yard was not prepared for any brick
in particular, but uniformly for all that are to be made.

   In the same way God has made this place of human habita-
tion for human beings, who are to be created and transferred
somewhere else after they have completed their time. And
just as the builder takes some bricks away so that newly made
ones can be put in their place, so God transfers by death, so to

speak, the earlier generations, and prepares a place for their successors.

A person who clings to this yard with his heart's affection, rather than taking the trouble to reflect constantly on the place to which he is to be transferred from here, is stupid, not to say insane.

Furthermore, it shouldn't seem unjust or harsh to the bricks when they are transferred hence, because it was for that reason that they were put here. It will only seem unfair or harsh to those who think they needn't be transferred from here, and who in their senseless greed claim as their own what is common property, belonging to no one but designated in general for countless people still to come.

Notice in this same situation another folly, no less than the first one: that although almost all these bricks are of the same size, yet scarcely one of them is content with the space a single brick needs—indeed each throws out or breaks as many bricks as it can, and claims for itself alone the place of many others.

408

Consider the fact that you entered this world turned away from God, gaping open-mouthed at everything but him.

409

Consider how miserable you are. From every direction you come across creatures that ensnare you with spurious blandishments and upset you with horrors. You are subjected to all of them because of the worthless burden of the flesh, to which they can make themselves either present or absent. And if only you loved them solely because of the needs of the flesh! Far more often it is because of your love for them that you do not use your body responsibly, when you either reject salutary things because they are less pleasant, or gladly receive harmful ones because they are pleasant.

410

What is this treasure that mice, fleas, lice and flies destroy?
For if what you say is true—'You are my portion, O Lord'—
either you don't need these transient things, or this, your portion, isn't enough for you. Every time you desire something
other than God, you declare either that you do not possess
him, or that he is not enough for you.

Ps 119(118):57, Mt 6:19–21

411

Notice how you are even worse than animals. Once replete,
they do not fend off other animals from what is left; but you
never stop grabbing and stockpiling even when you are full.

412

You avoid the same number of the devil's snares—and how
powerful they are—as you do transient delights—and how
strong they are, too! And you spurn as many medicinal remedies as the number of tribulations from which you flee, especially those that are in the cause of truth.

For *laqueos diaboli*, see 1 Tim 3:7, 6:9, and 2 Tim 2:26

413

To garnish something like food or drink solely in order to
make it more attractive is to co-operate with the devil for our
ruin, and to whet his sword so that it can penetrate our inmost
parts more easily and more deeply. The more we delight in
these things, the more seriously and deeply are we wounded.

Deut 32:41

414

You love foul-smelling goats for the sake of their milk, bees
for their honey and wax, dregs of olives for their oil, bunches

of grapes for their wine, manure for wheat. So when you love God for the sake of transient things, you treat him as a goat, a bee, olive dregs, bunches of grapes, and manure, and the transient things like milk, honey, wine, oil, and wheat.

415

You should be ashamed for having loved things that are bound to perish, and not get annoyed when they do.

416

First put yourself in the place of someone you want to judge or correct, and then do what you feel would be to your benefit if you were in his place. For 'the measure you give will be the measure you get, and with the judgment you pronounce you will be judged'. Christ first put himself in the place of man before judging him.

Mt 7:2

417

Let a person rejoice on finding a place where he can work in the hope of a reward that will endure; and let him summon there those he loves. Why, though? Because it is for God's sake that human beings should do good.

418

You should not even do something useful, such as making a knife from iron, for reasons of pride, nor should you do it for someone else who is motivated by that when he works. Do not glory in things like this, for thereby you avoid evil altogether. Only the person who does nothing for his own benefit should glory in what he does, and only he can do so—in other words, God himself.

419

For as long as it is for your own benefit that you do something for someone, you are doing it for yourself, not for him.

420

Show others, irrespective of the extent or the nature of their faults, the same attitude that you want God and other people to show you, irrespective of the extent or the nature of your offences.

421

Just as all things subsist through mutual resemblance and harmony, so all perish through mutual difference and discord.

422

The older and more ragged your shirt is, the less it matters to you what happens to it. Why don't you treat your flesh in the same way?

423

May the Lord be favorable to you, and not allow your mind to set foot somewhere, so that, if only under compulsion, O my soul, you may return to the ark, like Noah's dove.

Gen 8:8–9. Gregory the Great refers to *mentis membra* in his *Moralia in Iob* 1.2.4, and Augustine to *pes animae* in his *Enarr. in Psalmos* 9.15.

424

A mother who is hurt by her son does not seek revenge by hurting him, because she would regard that as hurting herself too. So if anyone were to hurt her son with the intention of avenging her, he should not be regarded as having revenged her, but as having hurt her a second time.

This is how every Christian ought to behave towards all. In other words, he should have compassion on someone who longs for what are the surest possible causes of pain for him— things that will perish.

425

Condemn what you long to conceal—your sin; and then there will not be anything you need to conceal. You can destroy sin, but you cannot conceal it. 'Nothing is covered that will not be revealed; nothing hidden, that will not be known.' Then why do you prefer to hide your sickness rather than heal it? You readily reveal your physical ailments to others so they can sympathize with you; and if they are reluctant to believe you, you think you are hard done by, you get more upset, and you even get angry with them. You should do the same thing with your spiritual ailments.

Mt 10:26

426

In the world to come, the saints will be wherever they want to be, for they will not want to be anywhere other than where they will actually be. The place will not bestow God: God will bestow the place. Knowledge and love will bestow God; but God bestows them—so God will bestow himself. Now a change of place may arise either from necessity or from a desire for pleasure. But no-one who possesses God will be able to find anything anywhere more conducive to his good, and more delightful. So I don't see why a person would want to change from one place to another.

427

You should look upon future events, which will necessarily come to nothing, as having already taken place, like past ones; and then consider what is left for you. Either there is God,

or there is nothing that can be known, considered, and said
to be good.

428

Look: if you love yourself, choose from these things what
is good for you. If you were well aware of the nature and
power of human opinion and partiality, you would never for
an instant work for them, rejoice in them, or mourn with
them—after all, they do no good to the one to whom they
are granted. But, just as colors and other physical forms either
disfigure or enhance the bodies or other things to which they
belong, so too these things—human partiality and opinion—
either enhance or disfigure the minds they infect and dwell
in, and either benefit or harm them.

For what good did it do to the sun or the moon that the
pagans thought of them as gods? What harm does the fact
that you know them to be creatures do to them? And even
if you were to think of them as dung, how would that hurt
them?

So, just as you explore the nature and power of this or
that herb or tree, do the same with these other things. With
God's help you can easily do this by assessing the opinions
and partialities of others by means of your own.

429

'It is good to hold fast to God'—for you, of course, not for
him. To depart from him is evil—again, for you, not for him.
So what are you frightened of, if you choose what is to your
advantage, and avoid what harms you? Even this, though, you
cannot do by yourself. 'Deliver me,' said Job, 'and set me
beside you.'

Ps 73(72):28, Job 17:3

430a

Take care that you do not despise the work of God on account of the work of man. The work of man is murder, adultery, and other such things. But the work of God is man himself.

430b

A person who loves something, such as a house or anything of that kind, also loves the material from which it is made, such as wood or stones. So everyone who loves good people must also love evil ones, from whom alone good people can come. Why should you not love something from which an angel can be made if you do love something from which a cup could be made? After all, it is written of people that 'they will be equal to the angels of God.'

Lk 20:36

431

If you must hate someone, it should be no one so much as yourself: no one else has done you so much harm.

432

You attach yourself improperly to created things in two main ways: either by leaning on them, like a kind of crutch for a sick person; or by enjoying them, as if they gave you good cheer.

433

Although there are many and divers things which a person should do for his fellow human beings, they should nevertheless be done not with many and divers intentions, but only with one; and that is the love that seeks their good.

434

Some love and experience God—in other words, justice and truth—in him, in God: others in truthful and just people.

435

Unless you set a low value on anything people can do, irrespective of whether they oppose you or help you, you won't be able to set a low value on their feelings—their hates, and loves; nor, for the same reason, on their opinions, good and bad alike.

436

You should not want to possess transient things, but to make good use of the ones you have. As Scripture says, 'He who makes haste to be rich will not be innocent'.

Prov 28:20

437

Since nothing can be closer to any given object than itself, and nothing more readily at hand, it is utterly astonishing that the human soul should be able to know something else better and more intimately than itself. If someone holding a knife or some other object in his hand starts looking for it, he certainly makes everyone watching him laugh. But what is so immediately at hand to the soul as itself? What can it know better, then, than itself? For that matter, how can it know anything at all, if it doesn't know itself?

438

Notice how you sell love and the other spiritual affections for pennies and small change, like wine in a tavern. And notice too how you buy opinions and loves and other spiritual affections or emotions for pennies and small change, like wine in a tavern.

439

When a person goes to sea on a voyage, all those who love him are frightened and in tears, even though only one danger appears to threaten him on his trip, and that is shipwreck. How much more should we fear and grieve for someone who enters this world, which happens whenever anyone is born? It can be the case that the person going to sea escapes the sea's dangers; but it is impossible for anyone entering the world to escape those of the world. How many physical dangers are there, to say nothing of the spiritual ones—and who can count them? As long as we live, then, not two or three of these dangers, but all of them, frighten us, since we are bound to die through one of them. It would be better for us to suffer from just one of them, and not fear the rest, rather than to be terrified of them all without any hope of escaping.

In all this, human misfortune is evident, because when people want to flee from dangers, they only save themselves for yet more dangers. Anyone who is thought to have escaped a fever has been preserved for suffering and death from paralysis or gout or some other illness; and instead of one danger, two or more befall him.

440

When a beetle is flying round looking at everything, it doesn't opt for something beautiful or wholesome or lasting, but settles down immediately on any fetid dung that may be lying around and rejects all the beautiful things. In the same way, your spirit flits around, looking at heaven and earth and all that is great and precious within them, but without attaching itself to any of them: despising them all, it gladly embraces all kinds of shoddy and sordid things that come into its thoughts. You should be ashamed of yourself for this.

441

The first task of a doctor, in treating a patient entrusted to him, is to diagnose and investigate the illness itself. His second task, after identifying the disease, is to apply appropriate remedies.

442

If you are happy when you experience the attributes and forms of physical bodies, such as their warmth and cold, sweetness and bitterness, then how much happier are the bodies themselves, which are actually like that, seeing that to be something is greater than to be affected by it? If you take the nature of something warm, the warmth itself is greater than the fact of being affected by it. So if it is good for you to be affected by it, it is even better to be the thing itself.

443

Some things are commanded by God because they are good for us, such as 'you shall love the Lord your God with all your heart,' and so on, this being the reason why happiness itself is ordained for us. Other things are good for us because they have been commanded, such as 'of the tree of the knowledge of good and evil you shall not eat'. This does not seem to have been commanded because it is good in itself, but for human beings to learn obedience by it. Even if it were not good in itself, it was still eminently good for us to be subject and obedient to God; and, to put it the other way round, even if it were not harmful to eat of that tree, it was nonetheless fatal to fight against God.

Mt 22:37, Gen 2:17

444

Someone who is grief-stricken and angry over the loss of some transient thing shows by doing so that he deserves to have lost it. Similarly someone who is angry or grief-stricken over being insulted shows that he deserved it. For he wanted to be praised just as much as he did not want to be insulted.

445

You do not doubt that carnal delights are bound to perish, and so should not be desired at all. That being the case, you should either desire nothing whatever, or thirst only for what is eternal.

446

The lover of the Creator is as different from the lover of a creature as the worshipper of the Creator is from the worshipper of a creature. I mean 'love' in the sense of 'enjoy' and 'rely upon', not in the sense of 'take care of', someone.

447

If nothing can be made any better without first being criticized, then someone who doesn't want to be criticized clearly does not want to be any better. It is written: 'He who yields to reproof possesses understanding.'

Prov 12:1, 15:32

448

Desire people's goodwill and approval in only one situation, that is, when you want to direct them towards what is genuinely good. So too a good and devoted doctor desires in certain circumstances the goodwill and approval of a patient, not of course for his own good, but for the good of the patient. Genuine good and genuine evil can never be conferred or imposed on someone against his will.

449

True salvation for anyone consists only in wanting, which means loving, what he should love, and wanting and loving it as much as he should. So, by contrast, true evil consists solely

in not wanting—that is, not loving—what he should, or in not
wanting or loving it as much as he should.

450

You are upset because you have been treated with contempt
and held in low esteem. By doing so you prove that you should
have been treated with contempt and held in low esteem, and
that it was right for this to happen. If you hadn't deserved
to be treated thus, you wouldn't have been at all frightened
or upset when it happened. Indeed, the very fact that you are
frightened and upset at the prospect of being treated with
contempt and held in low esteem shows that you are worthy
of such treatment. Without a shadow of doubt a person has
no fear of being considered worthless and despised unless he
deserves it.

451

When you have said and done everything, good and bad alike,
so as not to lose this life and to ensure that your body is neither killed nor destroyed, is there any way you can hold onto
it? Won't your body inevitably die soon, and be consumed
in a much worse and more hideous manner by worms than
could ever be achieved by human beings?

Are any of those who, at the time of the martyrs, denied the Lord for fear of death, still alive? Didn't they lose
everything—the Lord whom they denied, and this life and all
that belongs to it—for which they denied him? It might be
some consolation if, having lost God, human beings could at
least keep that for which they lost him.

452

If only you could distinguish what should be loved from what
shouldn't as easily as what is white from what isn't. Consider
this carefully.

453

One person gave all he had in return for popular acclaim, the other for the gratification of his throat and stomach. Whose action was worse? I really don't know; but I do know that the one acted with a pig's intentions, the other with the devil's.

454–5

(454) Although a nurse knows that a little child would be thrilled at being given a sparrow, she takes very great care to ensure that he doesn't get one, and all the more so as she thinks he would be delighted by it.

There is no denying the fact that everyone would like themselves and those they love to be happy. In which case, why does the nurse not only not want the child to have it, but also go to great lengths to ensure that he doesn't get it, as though it were a great evil? She certainly wants him to be happy. So why does she take away the very thing that is about to make him happy? Why, if not that she is alert to a future sadness whose cause she realizes will be precisely this enjoyment? For she knows very well that the boy's spirit will experience later a great sadness in direct proportion to the intense joy that preceded it: in fact she measures the amount of future sadness by the amount of present joy.

In so doing, what else does this woman advise us to do other than to avoid like plague and poison all forms of joy that are followed by tears, and to pay attention not to whatever pleasure they afford while they are with us now, but to whatever bitterness they engender in us when they go? For this is what all transient joys do.

Surely, then, for the same reason, and with a precautionary eye to the future, I should avoid possessing a vineyard, a meadow, a beautiful home, an estate—and avoid gold and silver, the opinions and praises of people, and similar things?

If only someone would give to that decrepit and yet stupid child, which is the human race throughout the world, some great, very wise and strong nurse, who with the same concern and anxiety might take or call him away from the joys which are the seeds of future sorrow!

And yet what causes so much tearful complaining throughout the world, if not the fact that this very devoted and powerful nurse never ceases, either herself or in some other way, to remove or withhold from the human race the transient things that cause its sufferings, like a sparrow from a child?

(455) Finally, what else do bishops or priests and other representatives of this nurse do when they teach, admonish, promise, threaten, receive into communion or even excommunicate, and exercise all their responsibilities, if it is not to recall that stupid child from his destructive delights? This is also what caused the quarrel between our bishop and the count. In effect, the count is the child, and the bishop plays the role of the devoted nurse. The sparrow is their bone of contention. But that child, stubborn because of his physical strength and the number of his partisans, has despised his nurse as someone weakened by illness and old age, and has enjoyed his destructive delights. As for the nurse, the more she loves him the more she grieves for him, not because she is jealous of his joy but because she takes into account the suffering that will follow.

Truly the world's sufferings are those of children mourning the loss of their sparrows!

The image of God as nurse is an unusual one. Guigo may have been influenced by Saint Paul's reference to himself as a nurse ('even as a nurse cherishes her children', 1 Thess 2:7), or by Saint Anselm's use of the image in referring to Saint Paul ('Prayer to Saint Paul', *The Prayers and Meditations of Saint Anselm*, trans. Benedicta Ward, SLG, (London: Penguin, 1973) p. 141. The quarrel alluded to here, between Count Guigo III of Albon and Hugh of Grenoble, ended in 1116. It is described in chapter 16 of Guigo's own *Life of St Hugh* (ed. Bellet: Montreuil, 1889).

456

Why do you want people to love you? 'Simply so they can be helpful to me in living my life.' That is to say, because you feel you are weak and ready to succumb to their power—as if you were to say: 'If people want, I shall die: if they wish it, I will live.' This is wrong, because you are bound to die, whether they wish it or not. What can you do, after all, to avoid dying? Thus you want people to have a high or good opinion of you, so that they will love or fear you. But let them love or fear you in order to do you good, or at least not to harm you. On the other hand you are frightened of, and dread, the idea that people should have a low or bad opinion of you, or hate, despise, or harm you, or at the very least do you no good.

All this, however, is the result of the experience of your own weakness and debility, which you have brought about by abandoning God and by clinging to and depending on weak and insecure things. If you didn't sense how worthless and weak they are, you would neither be frightened nor be upset because of them. But you do get frightened and upset when they perish or are taken away; and you do recognize and sense how worthless and weak they are, which is why you can offer no excuse whatsoever for loving them or depending on them.

Now it is quite astonishing to be aware of the weakness of something, and yet to depend on it: to know how worthless it is, and yet to love or admire it. So whenever you are upset or frightened because of these things, you prove that you have two attitudes which one would not think could possibly co-exist: you know and sense how weak and worthless these things are, and yet you love them and depend on them. If one of these attitudes were not present in you, if you either didn't love them or didn't know how worthless they were, you wouldn't suffer at all when they vanished.

457

A doctor is prevailed upon by many gifts and requests to agree to provide his prescriptions for someone who is dangerously ill. Yet God is despised when, without being rewarded or requested, he gives advice and prescriptions spontaneously to those in danger of eternal death.

I wonder what would happen if he were to prescribe for us things that were beneficial, not to us, but to him? If it is bad for a patient to disregard what a human doctor prescribes, how can it be good to despise the prescriptions of the divine physician? And if health is the result of following the prescriptions of a human being, how can it be lost by following the commandments of God?

458

People buy at great expense, and carry out with great effort and suffering, the prescription of a man who is giving temporal care to a body that is bound to perish, and who is often mistaken. People despise the prescription freely offered by God, who cares about the eternal salvation of an eternal soul, and who cannot be mistaken; and the one who offers this prescription has insults inflicted on him.

459

The secular authority promulgates laws, not out of a concern for people's good, but to serve its own interests; and these laws are feared so much that one would scarcely dare to violate them even in secret.

The laws of God are not promulgated for his good, but only for our salvation. They are neither feared like those of the powerful, nor loved like those of the altruistic, to the extent that they are publicly violated, and those who violate them brag about it.

460–1

(460) What reward does God give to the angels for serving him? Is it that of the Jews—a land flowing with milk and

honey? In which case, why do they serve him? Because it is good for them to hold fast to him.

If a human being, still clothed in mortal and frail flesh, could say to God 'What have I in heaven but you, and besides you what do I desire upon earth?', and 'It is good for me to hold fast to God', how much more are the angels able to say the same?

(461) God enjoined upon the Jews, as a heavy labor, human beings' highest good and the thing on which alone they should set their hearts: the worship of God. But what is most worthless and utterly despicable to human beings was promised as a reward: transient things.

For Christians it is the other way round: transient things, which were promised or given to the Jews as a reward, they were commanded to trample underfoot as dung; and the worship of God, which was laid upon the Jews as a labor, they were commanded to love.

Deut 6:3, Ps 73(72):25, Ps 73(72):28

462

Consider what it is that you should be concerned to improve. It shouldn't be the highest or most perfect things, because they cannot get any better. But neither should it be the most hopeless and lowest of things, because they too can never make any progress. It should, then, be things in the middle, those not yet so good that there is no room left for improvement, nor so bad that they are incapable of improvement.

463

Notice how, because you have not shown yourself to be wholeheartedly subjected to God, you are instead subjected to lice and little mice.

(464) Everything you see has, according to its kind, a certain natural beauty and perfection. When it lacks this, and is impaired in some way, it rightly displeases you. So, for example, if you happen to see someone with a mutilated nose, you at once recoil from it. You are aware of what he lacks in respect of the natural perfection of the human face. It is the same with everything, even with the leaf of a nettle, or of any plant you like.

Now who would deny that the human mind has a certain natural beauty and perfection that is peculiar to it? Indeed, so far as it is present, the mind is duly praised; and, so far as it is lacking, it is justly criticized.

Think, therefore, with God's help, how much of this beauty and perfection your own mind lacks, and never stop reproving yourself for this.

Cf. Ezek 23:25, where God prophesies the cutting-off of adulterous Israel's nose.

(465) What, then, is the natural beauty of the soul? It consists in being devoted to God. And to what extent? 'With all your heart, and with all your soul, and with all your mind, and with all your strength.' Furthermore, intrinsic to this beauty is goodwill towards your neighbor. To what extent? 'Even to death.'

But if you are not like that, whose will the loss be? Certainly not God's: perhaps to some extent your neighbor's; but undoubtedly yours most of all. For to be deprived of natural beauty and perfection must be harmful to something. If a rose ceases to be red, or a lily to be fragrant, this will seem some loss to me, as someone who loves pleasures of this kind; but for them, for the rose and the lily, being stripped of their natural and proper beauty is a much greater and more damaging loss.

Lk 10:27, Jn 15:13, Phil 2:8

(466) The true perfection of a rational creature consists in valuing each thing as it should be valued. It must be valued at its true worth, because to assess it at more or less than that is to go wrong.

Now everything is by nature either above, or beside, or below this rational creature. Above him is God, beside him is his neighbor, below him is everything else.

He must, therefore, value God as he should be valued. God is to be valued at his true worth; but unless he knows how great God is, he will not be able to value him at his true worth. Yet the extent of God's greatness can be known completely only by God alone; for his self-knowledge surpasses ours to the same extent as his being does.

So, then, just as our being is nothing when compared to his, so his self-knowledge makes ours by comparison into mere blindness and ignorance. Therefore only his self-knowledge is perfect and comparable to his nature, as our Lord said: 'No one knows the Father save the Son'.

So, just as only his understanding of himself is perfect in his eyes, so only his love of himself is entirely comparable and fitting to his nature. Indeed only he loves himself perfectly, according to his true worth, because only he knows himself perfectly.

Mt 11:27

(467) Return now to the definition which you set down at the beginning. After closer scrutiny it is incontestable that this applies not to the rational creature, but to God alone: leaving aside all the other beings, he and he alone, as we have seen, knows and loves himself as he really is.

In what, then, does perfection for the rational creature consist? It is this: to value all things—those above him (God), those beside him (his neighbor), and those below him (unreasoning animals and so on)—as they ought to be valued by him, in other words by a rational creature. Now collect your thoughts on how they are to be valued along these lines:

(468) Nothing is set above God, nothing is comparable to him, nothing regarded as equal either to a half, or a third, or even the tiniest part of him. The rational creature must value nothing more than him, nothing equal to him, nothing half as much, nothing even remotely as much, as him. He must love nothing more, nothing as much, nothing in proportion even to a tiny part, in comparison to him. Our Lord himself told us: 'You shall love the Lord your God with all your heart, and with all your soul, and with all your mind, and with all your strength'. In other words, you are to love nothing else for your joy and your support.

This is how you are to value the higher things.

Lk 10:27

(469) Now all people are naturally equal in respect of their nature. Therefore the rational creature ought to consider everyone as equal to himself. Just as he ought not to set himself above, or alongside, or as in any way equal to, the higher things—in other words, God—in love, neither should he do so with anyone else.

And just as he must not set anything of the lower order before his own salvation, or on a level with it, or as in any way equal to it, neither must he set anything before the salvation of anyone else. Whatever he has to do or suffer for his own eternal salvation, he must do or suffer for the salvation of everyone else. For, as the Lord said: 'You shall love your neighbor as yourself.'

This is how you are to value things that are your equal.

Cf. Gregory the Great, *Regula pastoralis* 2.6; PL 77:34: 'God has made all human beings equal by nature'; Mt 22:39.

(470) Lower things are those that come after the rational spirit: that is, the life of the senses, which he shares with cattle; animate life, which he shares with plants and trees; and the substance of the body, with its forms and attributes, which he shares with metals and stones. So, just as the rational creature should love nothing more than the higher things, nothing as much as them, and nothing in comparison to them, so also

he ought to consider nothing as being of less value than the lower things, nothing as slight, nothing by comparison as even in the smallest particular as worthless as they are. And this is what is written about them: 'Love not the world, neither the things that are in the world.'
This is how you are to value the lower things.

1 Jn 2:15. Cf. Gregory the Great, *Homilia in Evangelia* 29; PL 76:1214; CS 123:227: 'Stones have being, but neither life nor feeling. Plants and trees are alive, but they have no feeling . . . Brute animals exist, they are alive and have feeling, but they have no understanding. Finally angels exist. They are alive, possess feeling and understanding. Human beings have something in common with every creature. They share existence with stones, like trees they are alive, like animals, they feel, and like the angels, they have understanding.' This homily was read in the Carthusian night office.

(471) So such a person will have higher things for his delight, equal things for his companions, lower things for his servants. He will be devoted to God, kind to his neighbour, circumspect towards the world. He will be the servant of God, the companion of man, the lord of the world: set beneath God, not arrogant towards his neighbor, not subject to the world. He will restore the lower things for the well-being of the middle ones and the honor of the higher ones. He will be neither ungodly nor blasphemous nor sacrilegious towards the higher things; neither arrogant nor envious nor bad-tempered towards the things that are his equal; neither inquisitive nor profligate* towards the lower things. He will accept nothing from the lower, nothing from his equals, but everything from the higher things: marked with the imprint of the higher, he will mark the lower with his own imprint: moved by the higher, he will move the lower: influenced by the higher, he will influence the lower: following the higher, he will lead the lower: possessed by the former, he will possess the latter: restored by the former to their likeness, he will restore the latter to his.

flagitiosus: cf. Augustine, *De doctrina christiana* 3.10.16; CCSL 32:87: 'That which uncontrolled cupidity does to corrupt the soul and its body is called a "vice" (flagitium). . . .'

(472) We strive for this perfection in this life, even though we shall only possess it fully in the world to come. The more fervently we pursue it now, the more fully shall we possess it then.

Then there will be no impulse in the mind that does not come from God, none in the body that does not come from the soul—and thus there will be no impulse, either in soul or body, that does not come from God.

There will be no more sin, which is perversion of the will, nor punishment for sin, which is corruption, sorrow, and the destruction of the flesh.

The naked mind will cling to the naked truth, needing no words, no sacraments, no images, to comprehend it, and no models. There 'a man will teach his brother no longer, saying: "Know the Lord." For they shall all know me, from the least of them to the greatest of them, says the Lord'. For 'they shall all be taught by God'.

Jer 31:34; Jn 6:45; Cf. Jerome, Ep 52.5: 'Naked, I shall follow the naked cross', ed. Labourt 2:178

(473) If the soul were really pure, it would see for itself these outlines of virtue and justice even now, in this mortal life, in the very truth and wisdom of God.

It would also see that not only it, the human soul, will be immortal and eternal, but that its own flesh will be too, in the resurrection. And moreover it would clearly perceive that same resurrection there as well, in God who is both Word and Wisdom.

But because it could not do this, by reason of its own impurity, a human mind was added to the Word. This mind received the very Word of God in all his fullness; and, being completely conformed to him and made like him, it was marked fully and entirely by his imprint alone, as was written: 'Set me as a seal upon your heart'. So, entirely restored to his likeness (just as wax is fashioned to the likeness of a seal), the human mind might reveal the Word to us in itself, to be seen and known.

Yet we were so blind that not only were we unable to see the Word of God: we could not even see his human soul. That is why a human body was added too.

Song of Songs 8:6. Cf. Gregory the Great, *Moralia in Iob* 29:21; PL 76:488: 'Indeed the Lord made man, whom he fashioned into his own likeness, as a kind of seal of his power'.

(474) So there are these three: the Word of God, a human mind, and a human body. If we could see the first, we would not need the second; and if we could at least see the second, we would not need the third.

But because we could see neither the first nor the second, that is neither the Word of God nor the human mind, the third was added, that is, a human body. And so 'the Word was made flesh, and dwelt' with us, in our external world, so that in this way at least he might one day lead us into his inner world.

Jn 1:14

(475) And so it was that a rational soul, endowed with flesh, was added to the Word of God, so that through that same flesh the Word might teach, accomplish and endure whatever was necessary to instruct and correct us. In that soul alone existed to perfection the things we discussed above—that is, devotion to God, goodwill towards one's neighbor, and circumspection towards the world.

For he preferred nothing to God, compared nothing to him, and regarded nothing as equal to any part of him. He loved nothing more, nothing as much, nothing in proportion to any part of him whatever. And so he said 'I do his will always'—the will, that is, of the Father.

Furthermore he loved his neighbor perfectly, as he loved himself. He neglected none of the things below him—in other words, beneath the rational mind—but directed everything towards the good of his neighbor: the life of the senses, animate life, and the flesh itself. He endured for us the fiercest pains which assail the life of the senses; death, which assails our animate life; and the wounds that harm the flesh itself. Towards the world, however, he showed such great circumspection and contempt that the Son of man had nowhere to lay his head. He took for himself nothing from the lower things, nothing from the middle things, but everything from the higher ones—that is, from the Word of God to whom his soul was joined in a personal unity.

The soul of Christ was taught how to understand, and enkindled to love, not by sacraments, nor by words, nor by examples, but only by the presence of the Word of God. Through that presence the very Word and Wisdom of God revealed to us in three ways—by sacraments, words, and examples—what is to be done, what to be endured, and why.

Jn 8:29, Mt 8:20

(476) For man should only follow God, but could only follow man. Thus human nature was assumed, so that by following someone he could, he might also follow the one he should.

In the same way, it was good for man to be conformed only to God, in whose image he was made; but he could be conformed only to man. Thus God was made man, so that while being conformed to a man, which he could, he might also be conformed to God, which was good.

Cf. Gregory the Great, *Moralia in Iob* 24:2; PL 76:287: 'For sinful man could not be amended, except by God. But it was necessary that he who was healing him, should be an object of sight; in order that he might amend our former sinful lives, by setting a pattern for us to imitate. But it was not possible that God could be seen by man; He therefore became man, that he might be seen . . .' (English trans. in 'Morals on the Book of Job', Oxford: Library of the Fathers, vol. 5 [1897] 50–51). Cf. Augustine, *De Trinitate* 7.4 (CCSL 50:253); *Serm.* 380 (PL 39:1676); *Enarr. in Psalmos* 134.5; Mursell, *The Theology of the Carthusian Life*, Analecta Cartusiana 127 (1988) 134–6; Laporte, in SCh 308:311–312; Hocquard, *Les méditations . . .* , Analecta Cartusiana 112/2 (1987) 79–80.

Abbreviations

AOC	Annales Ordinis Cartusiensis (by Dom Charles Le Couteulx) (Montreuil, 1887)
BA	Bibliothèque Augustinienne (Paris, Desclée and Brouwer)
CC	*Consuetudines Cartusiae* of Guigo I
CCSL	*Corpus Christianorum Series Latina* (Turnhout: Brepols)
CS	Cistercian Studies series (Cistercian Publications, Kalamazoo, Michigan)
DLT	Darton, Longman and Todd, London
PL	*Patrologia Latina*, ed. J.-P. Migne
RAM	*Revue d'ascètique et de mystique*
SBOp	*Sancti Bernardi Opera*, edd. J. Leclercq and H. M. Rochais, 8 volumes, Rome: Editiones Cistercienses, 1957–1977
SC	Saint Bernard of Clairvaux, *Sermones super Cantica Canticorum* (Text in *Sancti Bernardi Opera* (see above); English translations in *Cistercian Fathers* series (Kalamazoo)
SCh	*Sources Chrétiennes* (Paris: Les Éditions du Cerf)

INDEX

Numbers without parentheses refer to pages. Numbers within parentheses refer to individual Meditations. Secondary authors whose works are referred to only in the notes are not included.

INDEX OF BIBLICAL REFERENCES

CISTERCIAN PUBLICATIONS, INC.
TITLE LISTING

CISTERCIAN TEXTS

THE WORKS OF
BERNARD OF CLAIRVAUX

Apologia to Abbot William
Five Books on Consideration: Advice to a Pope
Grace and Free Choice
Homilies in Praise of the Blessed Virgin Mary
The Life and Death of Saint Malachy the Irishman
Love without Measure. Extracts from the Writings
of St Bernard (Paul Dimier)
On Loving God
The Parables of Saint Bernard (Michael Casey)
Sermons for the Summer Season
Sermons on the Song of Songs I - IV
The Steps of Humility and Pride

THE WORKS OF
WILLIAM OF SAINT THIERRY

The Enigma of Faith
Exposition on the Epistle to the Romans
Exposition on the Song of Songs
The Golden Epistle
The Nature of Dignity of Love

THE WORKS OF AELRED OF RIEVAULX

Dialogue on the Soul
The Life of Aelred of Rievaulx by Walter Daniel
The Mirror of Charity
Spiritual Friendship
Treatises I: On Jesus at the Age of Twelve, Rule for
a Recluse, The Pastoral Prayer

THE WORKS OF JOHN OF FORD
Sermons on the Final Verses of the Songs of Songs I - VII

THE WORKS OF GILBERT OF HOYLAND

Sermons on the Songs of Songs I-III
Treatises, Sermons and Epistles

OTHER EARLY CISTERCIAN WRITERS

The Letters of Adam of Perseigne I
Baldwin of Ford: Spiritual Tractates I - II
Gertrud the Great of Helfta: Spiritual Exercises
Gertrud the Great of Helfta: The Herald of God's
Loving-Kindness
Guerric of Igny: Liturgical Sermons I - II
Idung of Prüfening: Cistercians and Cluniacs: The
Case of Cîteaux
Isaac of Stella: Sermons on the Christian Year
The Life of Beatrice of Nazareth
Serlo of Wilton & Serlo of Savigny
Stephen of Lexington: Letters from Ireland
Stephen of Sawley: Treatises

MONASTIC TEXTS

EASTERN CHRISTIAN TRADITION

Besa: The Life of Shenoute
Cyril of Scythopolis: Lives of the Monks of Palestine

Dorotheos of Gaza: Discourses
Evagrius Ponticus:Praktikos and Chapters on Prayer
The Harlots of the Desert (Benedicta Ward)
John Moschos: The Spiritual Meadow
Iosif Volotsky: Monastic Rule
The Lives of the Desert Fathers
The Lives of Simeon Stylites (Robert Doran)
The Luminous Eye (Sebastian Brock)
Mena of Nikiou: Isaac of Alexandra & St Macrobius
Pachomian Koinonia I - III
Paphnutius: A Histories of the Monks of Upper Egypt
The Sayings of the Desert Fathers
Spiritual Direction in the Early Christian East (Irénée
Hausherr)
Symeon the New Theologian: The Theological and
Practical Treatises & The Three Theological
Discourses
The Syriac Fathers on Prayer and the Spiritual Life
(Sebastian Brock)
The Wound of Love: A Carthusian Miscellany

WESTERN CHRISTIAN TRADITION

Anselm of Canterbury: Letters I - III
Bede: Commentary on the Seven Catholic Epistles
Bede: Commentary on the Acts of the Apostles
Bede: Homilies on the Gospels I - II
Conferences of John Cassian, I - III
Gregory the Great: Forty Gospel Homilies
The Meditations of Guigo I, Prior of the Charterhouse
(A. Gordon Mursell)
Guigo II the Carthusian: Ladder of Monks and
Twelve Meditations
Handmaids of the Lord: The Lives of Holy Women in
Late Antiquity and the Early Middle Ages (Joan
Petersen)
Peter of Celle: Selected Works
The Letters of Armand-Jean de Rancé I - II
The Rule of the Master

CHRISTIAN SPIRITUALITY

Abba: Guides to Wholeness & Holiness East & West
A Cloud of Witnesses: The Development of
Christian Doctrine (D.N. Bell)
Athirst for God: Spiritual Desire in Bernard of
Clairvaux's Sermons on the Song of Songs
(M. Casey)
Cistercian Way (André Louf)
Drinking From the Hidden Fountain (Spidlék)
Eros and Allegory: Medieval Exegesis of the Song of
Songs (Denys Turner)
Fathers Talking (Aelred Squire)
Friendship and Community (B. McGuire)
From Cloister to Classroom
Herald of Unity: The Life of Maria Gabrielle
Sagheddu (M. Driscoll)
Life of St Mary Magdalene and of Her Sister
St Martha (D. Mycoff)
The Name of Jesus (Irénée Hausherr)
No Moment Too Small (Norvene Vest)
Penthos: The Doctrine of Compunction in the
Christian East (Irénée Hausherr)
Rancé and the Trappist Legacy (A.J. Krailsheimer)
The Roots of the Modern Christian Tradition
Russian Mystics (S. Bolshakoff)
The Spirituality of the Christian East (Tomas Spidlík)
Spirituality of the Medieval West (André Vauchez)
Tuning In To Grace (André Louf)

CISTERCIAN PUBLICATIONS, INC.
TITLE LISTING

CISTERCIAN TEXTS

THE WORKS OF
BERNARD OF CLAIRVAUX

Apologia to Abbot William
Five Books on Consideration: Advice to a Pope
Grace and Free Choice
Homilies in Praise of the Blessed Virgin Mary
The Life and Death of Saint Malachy the Irishman
Love without Measure. Extracts from the Writings
    of St Bernard (Paul Dimier)
On Loving God
The Parables of Saint Bernard (Michael Casey)
Sermons for the Summer Season
Sermons on the Song of Songs I - IV
The Steps of Humility and Pride

THE WORKS OF
WILLIAM OF SAINT THIERRY

The Enigma of Faith
Exposition on the Epistle to the Romans
Exposition on the Song of Songs
The Golden Epistle
The Nature of Dignity of Love

THE WORKS OF AELRED OF RIEVAULX

Dialogue on the Soul
The Life of Aelred of Rievaulx by Walter Daniel
The Mirror of Charity
Spiritual Friendship
Treatises I: On Jesus at the Age of Twelve, Rule for
    a Recluse, The Pastoral Prayer

THE WORKS OF JOHN OF FORD

Sermons on the Final Verses of the Songs of Songs I - VII

THE WORKS OF GILBERT OF HOYLAND

Sermons on the Songs of Songs I-III
Treatises, Sermons and Epistles

OTHER EARLY CISTERCIAN WRITERS

The Letters of Adam of Perseigne I
Baldwin of Ford: Spiritual Tractates I - II
Gertrud the Great of Helfta: Spiritual Exercises
Gertrud the Great of Helfta: The Herald of God's
    Loving-Kindness
Guerric of Igny: Liturgical Sermons I - II
Idung of Prüfening: Cistercians and Cluniacs: The
    Case of Cîteaux
Isaac of Stella: Sermons on the Christian Year
The Life of Beatrice of Nazareth
Serlo of Wilton & Serlo of Savigny
Stephen of Lexington: Letters from Ireland
Stephen of Sawley: Treatises

MONASTIC TEXTS

EASTERN CHRISTIAN TRADITION

Besa: The Life of Shenoute
Cyril of Scythopolis: Lives of the Monks of Palestine

Dorotheos of Gaza: Discourses
Evagrius Ponticus:Praktikos and Chapters on Prayer
The Harlots of the Desert (Benedicta Ward)
John Moschos: The Spiritual Meadow
Iosif Volotsky: Monastic Rule
The Lives of the Desert Fathers
The Lives of Simeon Stylites (Robert Doran)
The Luminous Eye (Sebastian Brock)
Mena of Nikiou: Isaac of Alexandra & St Macrobius
Pachomian Koinonia I - III
Paphnutius: A Histories of the Monks of Upper Egypt
The Sayings of the Desert Fathers
Spiritual Direction in the Early Christian East (Irénée
    Hausherr)
Symeon the New Theologian: The Theological and
    Practical Treatises & The Three Theological
    Discourses
The Syriac Fathers on Prayer and the Spiritual Life
    (Sebastian Brock)
The Wound of Love: A Carthusian Miscellany

WESTERN CHRISTIAN TRADITION

Anselm of Canterbury: Letters I - III
Bede: Commentary on the Seven Catholic Epistles
Bede: Commentary on the Acts of the Apostles
Bede: Homilies on the Gospels I - II
Conferences of John Cassian, I - III
Gregory the Great: Forty Gospel Homilies
The Meditations of Guigo I, Prior of the Charterhouse
    (A. Gordon Mursell)
Guigo II the Carthusian: Ladder of Monks and
    Twelve Meditations
Handmaids of the Lord: The Lives of Holy Women in
    Late Antiquity and the Early Middle Ages (Joan
    Petersen)
Peter of Celle: Selected Works
The Letters of Armand-Jean de Rancé I - II
The Rule of the Master

CHRISTIAN SPIRITUALITY

Abba: Guides to Wholeness & Holiness East & West
A Cloud of Witnesses: The Development of
    Christian Doctrine (D.N. Bell)
Athirst for God: Spiritual Desire in Bernard of
    Clairvaux's Sermons on the Song of Songs
    (M. Casey)
Cistercian Way (André Louf)
Drinking From the Hidden Fountain (Spidlék)
Eros and Allegory: Medieval Exegesis of the Song of
    Songs (Denys Turner)
Fathers Talking (Aelred Squire)
Friendship and Community (B. McGuire)
From Cloister to Classroom
Herald of Unity: The Life of Maria Gabrielle
    Sagheddu (M. Driscoll)
Life of St Mary Magdalene and of Her Sister
    St Martha (D. Mycoff)
The Name of Jesus (Irénée Hausherr)
No Moment Too Small (Norvene Vest)
Penthos: The Doctrine of Compunction in the
    Christian East (Irénée Hausherr)
Rancé and the Trappist Legacy (A.J. Krailsheimer)
The Roots of the Modern Christian Tradition
Russian Mystics (S. Bolshakoff)
The Spirituality of the Christian East (Tomas Spidlik)
Spirituality of the Medieval West (André Vauchez)
Tuning In To Grace (André Louf)